Lectionary Tales
For The
Pulpit

---

57 Stories
For Cycle C

Richard A. Jensen

CSS Publishing Company, Inc.
Lima, Ohio

LECTIONARY TALES FOR THE PULPIT

Copyright © 1994 by
The CSS Publishing Company, Inc.
Lima, Ohio

Library of Congress Cataloging-in-Publication Data

Jensen, Richard A.
   57 lectionary stories for preaching : based upon the revised common lectionary, cycle C / Richard Jensen.
        p.   cm.
   I. Lectionary preaching. 2. Bible. N.T. Luke — Homiletical use. 3. Storytelling — Religious aspects — Christianity. I. Title. II. Title: Fifty-seven lectionary stories for preaching.
BV4235.L43J46   1994
251'.08—dc20   94-6759
                                                                        CIP

This book is available in the following formats, listed by ISBN:
0-7880-0081-0 Book
0-7880-0082-9 IBM (3 1/2 and 5 1/4) computer disk
0-7880-0083-7 IBM book and disk package
0-7880-0084-5 Macintosh computer disk
0-7880-0085-3 Macintosh book and disk package

PRINTED IN U.S.A.

To all who follow
*in Luke's train of thought as **narrators***
of the events that have been fulfilled among us.

Table Of Contents

Preface

I consider it a great honor and privilege to have been invited to produce this resource for your preaching. My earnest prayer is that you might find these stories useful in your preaching and that they may be found to be vehicles whereby God's abundant grace might touch the lives of your hearers.

I believe very much in the storytelling enterprise. My two works in the field of homiletical theory are titled: *Telling The Story* (1980) and *Thinking In Story*, CSS (1993). In the last section of the earlier work I advocated basically that a sermon could be a story! It would not need any explanation. That's how Jesus' parables worked. Gunther Bornkamm once said of Jesus' parables that, "the parables are the preaching itself." So I envisaged a kind of preaching where the *story was the preaching itself.*

This resource does not offer stories which can be the sermon itself. Herein are contained stories that you can "stitch together" with other stories to form a sermon. This is the approach to preaching that I have advocated more recently in *Thinking In Story.* What I know of "story stitching" I learned from those people who are the experts in the forms of communication in oral cultures. Thomas Boomershine helped me to wisdom here as well through his keen insight that the hermeneutic of an oral culture is to "think in story." Hence the title of my book.

In the book I propose that the shift from oral cultures to literate cultures was a shift from an age where people "think in story" to an age where people "think in ideas." Most homiletical thought in the past several hundred years has taught us to preach by lining up our points (usually three); by lining up our ideas. I am convinced that this form of preaching does not work well in the new communication environment in which we find ourselves today. Walter Ong and others have pointed out that there are many things about the communication patterns in this new age that are somewhat similar to the communication patterns of oral cultures. Both of these cultures, for example, communicate through *sound*. The world of print, on the other hand, is a *silent* world. In this "secondarily oral" culture of today, therefore, I strongly believe that one of the "new" ways to structure our preaching is to structure it by "stitching stories" together rather than through an outline of ideas.

"Thinking in story" sends us to our story resources. Our primary resources for stories for preaching are: 1) the Bible, 2) our own autobiography, 3) stories of individuals and communities of faith, 4) the arts and 5) stories of our own composing. The stories in this resource draw upon all of these sources. In my own preaching I have been increasingly drawn to the Bible as the primary resource for our preaching as storytelling. These are the stories that are normative in our communities of faith. These are stories our people hardly know! These are stories that have power in and of themselves! Through the telling of biblical stories God works still today to reach out and touch people's lives. I would urge you as you work your way through Luke's gospel to seek out other stories from Luke that can be "stitched together" with the text for the day to form a sermonic whole.

Sometimes, oftentimes, the best story you have from Luke is the text for the day. I have felt guilty at times in this writing process in offering you other stories to help illuminate the textual story. The textual story will be sufficient unto itself! Other stories we tell to help lift up the theme of a textual story always run the danger of becoming allegorical. That is, we tell a story that is basically a parallel story to the textual story. The textual story will do just fine by itself in most of these cases! Trust them! They are powerful! They don't need a lot of help from either one of us!

In my desire to entice you to tell more biblical stories, I have added a category to the usual format of this type of resource called *narrative analogy*. I first learned about "narrative analogy" from Robert Alter's book, *The Art of Biblical Narrative*. Alter is a professor of Hebrew and Comparative Literature at the University of California. He is a Jew. In his classic book he seeks to apply the kind of canons he uses to study literature in general to the Hebrew Bible. What Alter teaches us is that biblical stories "talk to each other." Parallel acts or situations are used to comment on each other in biblical narrative. He believes that the old world of Rabbinic Midrash knew this instinctively. Alter argues that some Midrashic scholarship that goes back 1,500 years, therefore, understands biblical narratives better than modern scholarship does. The reason for this is that this ancient form of biblical commentary operated with the assumption that a text in a narrative setting is *intricately interconnected with other stories in that narrative.* In other words, those old rabbinic scholars still knew how to "think in story." "Thinking in story," after all, is the way most of the biblical writers think!

Our gospels in the New Testament are narratives. The writers of these narratives "think in story." Their stories form an interconnected whole. Stories comment upon other stories. The so-called meaning of a story is highlighted by another story or stories! This is *narrative analogy.* In my preparation of the stories in this resource I have also tried, by using the category of narrative analogy, to *suggest other Bible stories* that you can tell in your sermon that help to elucidate the text at hand. The best commentary to help you with this task is Robert C. Tannehill's, *The Narrative Unity of Luke-Acts: A Literary Interpretation.* I highly commend it to you.

At times I have gone beyond suggesting narrative analogy and have put together a biblical story from another part of Luke that comments in some way upon the given text. These were cases where the evidence seemed overwhelming to me that the best story would be another story from Luke.

Wherever I quote the Bible in putting together a biblical narrative for your use I have quoted from the New Revised Standard Version of the Bible.

God's blessings be with you in your telling of the stories. Stories are the best tool you have today in reaching out to touch the human heart with the "amazing grace" of our Savior, Jesus Christ.

Richard A. Jensen

Advent 1
Psalm 25:1-10

Glenda Finds An Advent Prayer

It had been a tough week for Glenda Kruse. Glenda was a real estate agent and she had sold only one home during the entire month of November. She was getting desperate. She had to make a living after all.

Desperation, of course, is not very good for people. That week it had not been good for Glenda Kruse. On Wednesday evening she had an appointment to show a 10-year-old home to a family that was moving into the community. Herb and Mabel Daly were moving to town. Herb was coming to work at the telephone company and Mabel would be looking for work in the school system. Mabel had called the real estate office to inquire about a home they had seen advertised in the daily paper. Glenda Kruse got the call from her office to meet the Dalys at 7 p.m.

Eventually 7 p.m. came. Glenda and the Dalys showed up almost simultaneously at 1359 S. Linden. Glenda saw in the Dalys, of course, an opportunity for a sale! She began showing them around the ranch style home. Glenda knew that though the house was not that old the previous owners had let some things run down pretty badly. She was bound and determined this one time, however, to smooth over the rough spots about the house. She accentuated the positive. When the Dalys asked questions about certain items which Glenda knew were not in good repair she managed to talk her way around the problems. This was not Glenda Kruse's normal way of doing business. But this week she was desperate. She just had to make this sale. She stretched the truth pretty far in her presentation. And it worked. The Dalys signed an offer sheet on the house.

Glenda took the offer with a mix of emotions. It was good to be on the verge of a sale. It was not so good that she had compromised her own principles in the process.

As is so often the case in matters like these, Glenda Kruse got caught red-handed in her duplicity. The Dalys got an independent inspector to go through the house the next day who found all of the flaws Glenda had talked her way around. The Dalys were furious. They took back the offer on the home and asked that the real estate agency discipline Glenda Kruse for her unethical conduct.

It had indeed been a tough week for Glenda Kruse. She was almost ashamed to go to her church that Sunday morning. Glenda was pretty regular at church. She was there this Sunday and feeling awful. What had come over her anyway? How could she do such a thing? It just wasn't right. Glenda prayed silently, reflecting on her life. She thought about other aspects of her life as well. Not a pretty picture! She sat there in a mild state of depression. Things had to turn around in her life and soon. She needed a new start. She needed to write a new page in her life.

Glenda sat and stewed. She fumbled with the pew Bible in her hand. Her eyes caught sight of a Psalm verse that expressed her hope for the new in a wonderful way. "Be mindful of your mercy, O Lord, and of your steadfast love, for they have been from of old. Do not remember the sins of my youth or my transgressions; according to your steadfast love remember me, for your goodness; sake, O Lord!" (Psalm 25:6-7).

Glenda was ready for worship now. She was ready for God to come in mercy and make a new start with her life.

Advent 2
Luke 3:1-6

A Hostage Repents

Narrative Analogy: *Luke 1:5-80; 3:7-22*

Terry Anderson is probably the best known of the American hostages kept in Lebanon. Anderson, an Associated Press journalist, was held hostage for 2,454 days! His ordeal began innocently enough on March 16, 1985. As he dropped off his tennis partner after a morning match he noticed a green Mercedes pulled up just ahead of where he was stopped. Suddenly three young men came charging out of the car. Each had a 9-mm pistol hanging loosely on their hip. In a flash they were at Anderson's car window. "Get out," one of the men shouted. "I will shoot." Anderson got out. He was pressed into the back seat of the Mercedes and whisked away. The hostage ordeal for Terry Anderson had begun.

Anderson's first days of captivity were appalling. He was blindfolded most of the time. Held in chains. Interrogated roughly. His mind did not know how to react. Anderson realized that he was on the edge of madness. He was losing control of his capacity to think. "I can't do this anymore," he finally told his captors. "You can't treat me like an animal. I am a human being." When asked what he wanted he replied that he wanted a Bible. Not long afterwards a heavy object landed on his bed. He pulled down his blindfold. It was a Bible. He began to read. In Genesis!

Terry Anderson had been raised in the Catholic Church. Even though he had not been a practicing Catholic for years, however, the Bible came to him as a gift from heaven. He read. He pondered his life. He had lots of time to ponder his life. Too much time to ponder his life. He began a litany of confession in his mind. He confessed that he had hurt his first wife and daughter. He had made many mistakes. He had been a very arrogant person. He wasn't sure that people liked him much. He wasn't sure he liked himself very much.

Later in the first year of his captivity Anderson became aware of the fact that other hostages were living next door. One was a priest. Father Lawrence Jenco. He asked his captors if he could see the priest. "I am a Catholic," he told them. "I want to make a confession."

His wish was granted. Father Jenco came to his room. They both took off their blindfolds. Anderson hardly knew where to begin. It had been 25 years since he had last made confession. Father Jenco was encouraging. Anderson began reciting to this priest the sins he had been reflecting upon. There was much to confess. A bad marriage. Chasing women. Drinking. Anderson found it a very emotional experience. When he finished both he and Father Jenco were in tears. Father Jenco then laid his right hand upon Anderson's head. "In the name of a gentle, loving God, you are forgiven," the priest proclaimed.

Terry Anderson's faith deepened immensely in his hostage years. This moment of confession with Father Jenco, however, was his first formal step back into the church. Self reflection had grown within him out of the darkness of his hostage encounter. It was time to face the light. It was time in his life for a *turn around*.

The Case Of A Grocery Store Fix

It happened just about every time she went shopping for groceries. The check-out line always did her in. While Doris Watson was waiting her turn in line she could not keep her eyes off the covers of the many magazines placed strategically to capture attention. The covers captured her attention all right. She almost always grabbed one or two magazines off the rack to add to her pile of carefully selected groceries. Buying too many magazines. This was Doris Watson's "grocery store fix."

Doris Watson's "grocery store fix" had been part of her life for years. It was her way of coping with the messages our culture sends to women — messages which demand perfection: perfect hair, perfect make-up, perfect body and on and on and on.

The covers always reminded Doris of her many imperfections. One day, for example, she saw a cover which announced the latest hairstyles. Hair had been one of her downfalls. She wasn't blessed with beautiful hair. Keeping her hair looking decent took lots of work. Even though she wasn't always sure that the time she spent on her hair did the trick. Her husband certainly never seemed to notice unless the change in style was pretty marked. Doris took his indifference to mean a certain lack of perfection. She would have to try again. She was always on the lookout, therefore, for the latest word on hairstyle. When a magazine cover seemed to promise that the new styles were the best ever she bought it every time. Someday, perhaps, she would get it right.

And it wasn't just hairstyle that made Doris Watson anxious about her imperfections. Weight. That was always a problem. She always seemed to be at least five to ten pounds overweight. She saw all those perfect bodies on television and knew that she did not measure up. But what to do? How to lose weight? Goodness knows she had tried. The magazines raced to fill this gap as well. During the course of the year just about every magazine she spotted in the check-out line had a new dieting plan to follow. Doris Watson nervously bought them all. One of these weight reduction programs had to work. When it did she would have a body beautiful to behold.

Romance was another area in which Doris Watson succumbed to her "grocery store fix." The headlines constantly announced "Six Ways To Rekindle The Flame," "What To Do When The Love Seems Gone" and many other intriguing titles. She bought just about every one of those magazines. It wasn't that her marriage was all that bad necessarily. But it wasn't perfect and the message of the magazines was that it should be perfect and that it could be perfect. The magazine's demand for perfection always made her just a little bit tense. Maybe this time she would get it right.

Doris' husband made fun of her "grocery store fix." Once he really let fly at her. "You don't really expect these magazine articles to help anything do you," he would rail. "They're just trying to make a buck and they're making lots of them with you."

"Okay!" Doris would say. And she meant it. Somewhere deep inside herself she knew that her husband was probably right. But her resolve seldom worked. The next time she was in the grocery story those magazine covers would once again play on her insecurities. Such anxiety can prolong a "grocery store fix" for a long, long time.

Advent 4
Luke 1:47-55

The Wretched Of The Earth

Narrative Analogy: *1 Samuel 2:1-10; Luke 1:5-80; Luke 4:14-21*

"Look down and see the beggars at your feet. Look down and show some mercy if you can. Look down and see the sweepings of the street. Look down, look down upon your fellow man!" Thus reads the text of a song from the most popular work of musical theater in history: *Les Miserables*. In the musical version of the classic French novel by Victor Hugo this song shifts the scene to the squalid streets of Paris: 1832. It is sung by "the miserable ones," those from whom the novel and the musical takes its name. The beggars, the poor, the dregs of society sing to the upper crust. "Look down," they cry. "See our misery." Theirs is a cry as old as human history and as fresh as today's headlines. The world has always been filled with "the miserable ones," "the wretched of the earth," crying out for mercy and justice.

Soon after this cry of the wretched ones in *Les Miserables* the student revolutionaries swing into action on their behalf. These young idealists are out to see that justice is done. They sing together these words: "Do you hear the people sing? Singing the songs of angry men? It is the music of a people who will not be slaves again!" The revolutionary youth go on to sing of "life about to start when tomorrow comes." A word of hope appears in the midst of human wretchedness. It is the word of hope that has been held tight by "the miserable ones" in every generation of human history. This theme of *Les Miserables* strikes a universal human chord. People in every age have cried out for a better life. It is no wonder that this story takes such a firm grip on our human heartstrings. Hope for "the wretched of the earth" lives deeply in the hearts of human beings in every generation.

As is so often the case, however, those who fight for the new world that tomorrow brings are slaughtered on the barricades. The women sing of their grief at seeing their young men dead on the battlefield. "They were schoolboys," the women sing, "never held a gun ... Fighting for a new world that would rise up with the sun. Where's that new world now the fighting's done? Nothing changes. Nothing ever will ... Same old story. What's the use of tears? What's the use of praying if there's nobody who hears?" Nothing changes. Nothing ever will. Despair grips "the miserable ones" once more. There seems to be no hope. No point of tears.

And yet the final chorus of the musical dares yet to proclaim hope for "the wretched of the earth." The last words sung by the chorus ask if we hear the distant drums. These drums pound out the hope for the future that will come with tomorrow. "Tomorrow comes!" These are the last bold words of "the wretched ones." These are the last bold words sung in *Les Miserables*. "Tomorrow comes!"

And such it has been and such it will ever be. The poor, the lowly, the hungry can only dare to face life each day if there be some such ray of hope. Tomorrow! That hope beats with mighty strength in the lives of all this world's wretched ones. It might be that tomorrow the whole world will be turned upside down and justice will reign at last. Tomorrow — surely — our tears will be heard!

Christmas Eve
Luke 2:1-14

To You Is Born

Narrative Analogy: *Luke 1-2*

It was to be her first starring role. This year, at the Christmas pageant at Bethlehem Congregation, eight-year-old Tanya Baird was to play her first part. The kids in Tanya's third grade Sunday school class were to recite the Christmas story from Luke 2:1-14. They divided up the 14 verses so each student would have just a short part to learn. Tanya got to recite part of the words of the angels. "Do not be afraid; for see — I am bringing you good news of great joy for all the people: to you is born this day in the city of David a Savior, who is the Messiah, the Lord."

Samantha Baird, Tanya's mother, was so proud of her little girl. There was just one problem: her husband. Bill Baird hardly ever went to church. He had grown up in a family that believed in church — for the children. His parents took him to Sunday school every week. Either his dad or his mom would take him there and pick him up after class. Bill decided fairly early on in life that when it was up to him to make a decision about church he would shut all this church stuff out of his life. And he did.

Samantha Baird, on the other hand, had been pretty regular at church all of her life. It was because of her efforts that Tanya had been enrolled in Sunday school at the earliest possible age. Bill Baird tolerated this arrangement but he wasn't very happy about it. He just couldn't see the point. What did all this stuff have to do with anything real anyway? What did all this church stuff have to do with him?

Samantha Baird worked very hard the week before the program. She worked hard with Tanya helping her learn her

21

part. She worked hard with husband Bill trying to convince him he should go to the pageant. "For Tanya's sake, honey," Samantha Baird pleaded, "for her sake please go along just this once." At just that moment Tanya passed through the room. "Be not afraid; for behold, I bring you good news of a great joy . . . ." Her words trailed off as she passed through the living room.

"I don't see any point in going. I'd feel like a hypocrite," Bill Baird said after the interruption. "Just go as the video technician," Samantha pleaded. "Wouldn't it be great to have Tanya's first part on tape."

". . . for to you is born this day a Savior . . . ." Once again Tanya's words interrupted her parents' conversation. It was like that in the Baird home all week long.

Well, Bill Baird decided he would go along as video technician. He could justify that he thought to himself. Samantha was happy. Tanya was happy, too. And Tanya said her part splendidly. Everybody said so. It was a great pageant. The Baird family drove home that night as one big happy family.

For days to come the glow of the pageant filled the air of the house. Tanya also continued to fill the air of the house with her part. ". . . for to you is born this day in the city of David a Savior, who is the Messiah, the Lord," Tanya announced as she walked through the kitchen. Bill Baird listened with pride. And then it struck him. "*To you* is born this day . . . ." This Christmas announcement of the angels was addressed to him! "To you is born . . . ." In the Baird household this Christmas turned out to be the greatest Christmas of them all.

Christmas Day
John 1:1-14

A Baby Wrapped In Diapers

HBO hit the jackpot! The ratings they achieved for their special on Michael Jackson were awesome. The program aired about four years ago — before Michael's fall from grace. The special itself was to be a replay of an actual performance of Michael in Bucharest. Before that part of the program came on, however, there were 20 minutes of video hype introducing the audience to Michael Jackson. There were video clips of the great moments in his life. There were scenes from many of his concerts with young women screaming in delight, young men and women passing out from sheer excitement, fans of all ages adoring this young singer.

Pastor Grace Larsen watched the special with several members of her family. Pretty soon she started listening to what people in the room were saying about this prelude to Michael's appearance. "They treat him as if he were God," said her daughter. "Is he real?" someone else wondered out loud. Another said, "Bigger than life. Most definitely!"

This conversation got Pastor Larsen's attention. She started to pay closer attention to the way in which the appearance of this singing idol was presented. They really did treat him like a kind of god. He was bigger than life. The imagery was often quite blatantly religious. Much of the music under the video introduction sounded very much like sacred music from the past. Michael Jackson himself was shown several times in a pose that matched the position of Jesus on the cross. As the minutes ticked down to actual concert time, fire and smoke appeared as the mantle of his coming. Fireworks shot off. Spotlights danced with light. There was a hint of stardust in the air.

At long last Michael Jackson appeared in the flesh. His clothes enhanced his appearance. He stood immobile. The crowd went wild. They were in ecstasy. They seemed to worship the image. They adored the very presence of Michael Jackson. And it went on like that for the entire concert.

Pastor Grace watched the program unfold, paying particular note to its religious overtones. She didn't know many of the songs that Michael performed. Two songs at the end of the concert, however, really got her attention. One song sang about the challenge before all people to make the world a better place. The final song was a song Jackson had written called "Man in the Mirror." The theme of the song is that we can only make this world a better place if we look at ourselves in the mirror, and change our ways.

After this song concluded Michael Jackson got dressed in an astronaut's suit. With a power pack strapped to his back he blasted off from the stage in a burst of fireworks. "Mr. Jackson has left the stadium," the announcer said.

Pastor Larson thought and thought about the performance she had just seen. She liked it that Michael Jackson had appealed to all people to change their ways and change the world. She was disturbed, however, with the way he was portrayed. "They treat him as if he were God," her daughter had said. Pastor Grace thought about that line a lot while she was preparing her Christmas sermon. She played out the contrasts between the nearly "godlike" appearance of Michael Jackson and the appearance of the real God-made-flesh in Jesus Christ. There was no fire and smoke on the first Christmas night. Just a baby wrapped in diapers. There were no fireworks that shot off. Just a baby wrapped in diapers. No spotlights danced with light. Just a baby wrapped in diapers. There was no hint of stardust in the air. Just a baby wrapped in diapers. That's how it was when God became flesh to dwell among us, Pastor Grace thought to herself. Just a baby wrapped in diapers.

New Year's Day
Matthew 25:31-46

When I Saw Your Face

The New Year's Eve party at the Campbells' was always a highlight of the year for Tom Stone. The Campbells really knew how to throw a party. This year's party had been no exception. As the old saying goes, "A good time was had by all."

When the party was over in the wee hours of the new year Tom Stone walked home. The neighborhood Tom lived in was safe enough though it was boundaried by some pretty tough places. On his way home from the Campbells' he had to walk right through one of those troubled places. Tom walked gingerly now. He kept his eyes peeled in all directions for any signs of trouble. He didn't see any! He was almost through the rough spot when he thought he saw what looked to be a man's body on the street ahead.

Tom walked carefully. What to do? Dare he get involved with this beaten man in this godforsaken place? His mind flashed back to the New Year's Eve party at the Campbells' house. When someone asked him what his New Year's Resolution was he had said he would like to be a more caring person. It was like God planted this beaten body on the streets of his city to test his New Year's resolve to care. But a resolution is a resolution. Tom would see what he could do for the man.

Slowly and carefully, therefore, Tom made his way over to the beaten man. The beaten man didn't make a move. It looked like he had been severely beaten, stripped of his clothes, and robbed. His only communication was groaning sighs. Tom looked at the beaten and wounded and naked man and had compassion. Using a nearby telephone he called for a taxi cab. He accompanied the man to the emergency room of the nearest hospital. Once he could see that the man would be well taken care of he went home at last.

When Tom finally awoke the next afternoon his first thoughts were of the man he had encountered the night before. He decided he ought to go to the hospital and see how he was doing. So, off to the hospital he went. When he came into the man's room there was silence at first. The man was awake now and well on his way to recovery.

"I recognize your face," the beaten man whispered hoarsely. "You're the man who helped me last night. When I saw your face then I thought it must be the face of Jesus."

Tom mulled these words over in his mind not knowing just what to say. He rehearsed for himself the reason that he had stopped to help this man the night before. It was the New Year's resolution, of course. And it was even more particular than that. He had vowed to be a more caring person. He had vowed to serve Jesus in Jesus' time of need. A passage from Matthew's gospel haunted his consciousness. "Inasmuch as you did it to the least of these my brothers and sisters, you did it to me," Jesus had said. That's why he had stopped to help the beaten man.

Tom was lost in his thoughts on these matters when the man in the bed whispered again: "When I saw your face I thought it must be the face of Jesus."

"No," Tom replied, "it's quite the other way around. When I saw your face in that godforsaken place and heard your groanings and found you beaten, wounded, stripped naked and robbed I thought you must be Jesus."

Baptism Of The Lord
Luke 3:15-17, 21-22

Jesus Must Be A Real Person!

Narrative Analogy: *Luke 3:23-28*; 4:1-13 (cf. v. 3, 9); 4:16-22*

A missionary worked some years ago among a very primitive group of people in Papua New Guinea. This missionary worked under very difficult conditions. His world and the world of those for whom he translated the Bible were two very different worlds. In order to help bridge these worlds the missionary translator always worked with a language helper. First the missionary would make his translation. Next he would share his translation with his helper. If the language helper thought the translation was adequate he would in turn read it to his people to get their reactions to the material.

One day as his translation task was proceeding, the missionary made an amazing discovery. He had shown some photographs of places in the Holy Land in order to undergird his translating work. The people were surprised that the events of Jesus' life took place here on earth. They had believed these stories all to be true only of the spirit world.

And then an even more astonishing event of translating took place. The missionary was translating one of the four gospels. The genealogical list given in the gospel seemed to the missionary to be quite extraneous and beside the point. So he skipped over the genealogy and went on with the other translating. At the end, however, the missionary had to translate the genealogical list. It was a result of this translating event that the astonishing thing happened.

The missionary translator read his translation to his language helper fully expecting him to be bored to death with the whole thing. The helper was not bored at all. Rather, he promptly announced to the missionary that a very important

.

meeting was to be held that night so that the missionary might read today's translation to as many people as possible.

When evening time came the appointed house was completely full of people. The missionary had never seen so many people attend a Bible reading event before. The language helper asked the missionary to read his translation for the day. The missionary began to read name after name after name. As he read he realized that something strange was happening. The crowd of tribespeople was crisply attentive. They closed in upon him as he read. He was actually afraid they might crush him. He was afraid that what he was reading must have offended some ritual taboo about which he knew nothing. Perhaps they were angry with him. And he had no way to escape. He forced himself to keep on reading the names.

When the missionary translator had finished reading one of the men said to him: "Why didn't you tell us all this before? No one bothers to write down the ancestors of spirit beings. It is only real people who keep track of their genealogy." *"Jesus must be a real person!"* another voice cried in astonishment. "His genealogy is longer than ours!", cried out another. Still another said, "Jesus must have been a real man on this earth. He's not just white man's magic!"

What the missionary translator took to be a boring and meaningless list convinced these people that night that the truth of scriptures could no longer be in doubt. Jesus must be a real person! A real person *and* Son of God!

*This week's story is based on this text which is a commentary on Luke 3:15-17, 21-22.

The Holy Spirit Doesn't Have A Copy Machine

The wind of the Spirit blew through St. Mary's Parish but it did not seem to touch the life of Maria Sanchez. Maria had been a faithful member of St. Mary's Parish all of her life. She was baptized there, confirmed there, married there. And yet, when the Spirit blew new life into the lives of so many in the parish, Maria felt excluded.

Some called this blowing of God the "charismatic movement." Whatever it was called it certainly touched the lives of some of the members of St. Mary's in very special ways. Some spoke in tongues for the first time in their lives. Others spoke words of prophecy while others interpreted prophetic words and still others experienced the power of healing.

Maria Sanchez knew these people whose lives had been touched by God in new ways. She was excited for them. She joined them in some of their special prayer meetings. Maria's friends knew of the depth of her faith. This was not in question, at least not in the beginning. Maria was welcomed into their fellowship. She was excited to be there. She experienced the gifts of the Spirit as others exercised them. None of these new gifts were manifested in her life, however. That's where the problem arose.

Maria's newly "spirit-filled" friends wanted to pray for her with the laying on of hands so that she might also be filled with the Spirit and experience the work of God's Spirit in her life in new ways. Maria was more than willing to be prayed for. So the prayer fellowship prayed for Maria. They prayed — but nothing happened. No new gifts of the Spirit, that is, became manifest in Maria's life.

They prayed for Maria at the next meeting as well. And the next and the next and the next! But — nothing! It seemed to Maria that the matter got focused on the gift of speaking in tongues. "Everyone ought to have this gift," the others told her as they prayed and prayed for her. "Speaking in tongues is a sign of increased holiness," they told Maria.

The prayers did not seem to work, however. Maria Sanchez did not speak in tongues. She did not prophesy nor interpret prophetic utterances nor acquire new and greater faith nor experience new healing power. All the prayers seemed to be in vain. Maria Sanchez experienced all of this as a source of great guilt. What was the matter with her? What was wrong with her faith life? Why couldn't she speak in tongues? In the company of her "spirit-filled" friends she could only see herself as a spiritual failure.

One day Maria's aunt came to visit her. Maria knew her Aunt Carmen to be a woman of great faith. Maria told her aunt of her experiences with her spiritual friends and of her own despair over God's lack of presence in her life. Aunt Carmen heard Maria's story of pain and replied in great wisdom. "The Holy Spirit has been at work in your life ever since you were baptized," Aunt Carmen began. "It is the Spirit that has taught you to have faith in Jesus. It is the Spirit that has given you your many gifts for the common good of God's people. The Holy Spirit doesn't have a copy machine. Only you have been given the gifts that you have. The Spirit doesn't want you to be like anyone else. The Spirit gives each one of us a different assortment of gifts. Our spiritual task is to use the gifts the Spirit gives us for the common good."

Epiphany 3
1 Corinthians 12:12-31a

The Greater Honor

It was to be "Spiritual Gift" Sunday in Corinth of old. After all it was no lesser an authority than Paul himself who had said of these people that they were, ". . . not lacking in any spiritual gift" (1 Corinthians 1:7). Not lacking indeed! They were abounding in spiritual gifts and once every year they gathered in their worship service to honor the greatest among them.

On "Spiritual Gift" Sunday it was the custom that a man named Theo conduct the ceremony of honoring. Theo had worked hard with his assistants to construct a series of podiums in the front of the church building. Theo stood next to the lowest podium. He announced to the congregation in a solemn voice: "Will all those who have one gift of the Spirit please come forward and stand here." Everyone knew what this meant. There was a kind of approved list of special gifts of the Spirit in Corinth. Theo's invitation was for all who had at least one of these special gifts to come forward and stand on the lowest platform. And the people came.

Theo was now ready for his second announcement. He moved to the next highest platform. "Will all those who have two gifts of the Spirit please come forward." Theo then moved to the next highest platform. "Will all those who have three gifts of the Spirit please come forward," he called out. More people came forward filling the third highest platform. "Spiritual Gift" Sunday proceeded as Theo called forward those who had four gifts of the Spirit, then five, then six, then seven, then eight, then nine. Those with nine gifts of the Spirit stood on the highest platform.

The honoring was now visually complete. Everyone in the congregation could see just how people rated in spiritual

31

giftedness. The greatest honor, the highest platform, was for those with the most gifts. The lowest honor, the lowest platform, was for those with only one gift. Even they, however, were better off than the people who seemed to have no gifts at all. Those who appeared to have no special gifts could only remain in the congregation and gaze in honor at the wonderful array of spiritually gifted people standing before them. There they stood. In plain view. From top platform to bottom. What a sight! What an honor to be among the spiritually gifted. "Spiritual Gift" Sunday was certainly one of the highlights of each year in this congregation in Corinth so very long ago.

And then the bubble burst. Just after the ceremony honoring the spiritually gifted was complete the president of the congregation read the latest letter from Paul. It was always exciting to hear from this great missionary who had once served in Corinth. Some of the things Paul had to say in his letter, however, deeply disturbed the spiritual leaders of the congregation. Theo, for one, just walked out of church upon hearing some of Paul's advice. When the reading of the letter was finished and the service ended Theo headed straight for the exit.

Outside the church Theo quickly gathered around himself those who had stood on the ninth step. Theo and the others just shook their heads over Paul's letter. Theo said, "I thought I had heard more than I could take and then those cruelest words of all." Theo spat those words out in disgust: " 'Give the highest honor to the inferior part.' It's crazy," Theo said. "That would put an end to our "Spiritual Gift" Sunday altogether. Paul turns honoring upside down!"

Epiphany 4
1 Corinthians 13:1-13

The Greatest Of These

In the midwest the summer of 1993 was the summer of the "great flood." The rains, it seemed, would never cease. Rivers all across the central section of our land broke from their banks, broke through retaining walls and laid waste to ten thousands of acres of farmland and many cities besides. It was a summer of horror for great numbers of our citizenry. Many of them lost just about everything they had.

Tom and Donna Starr manage several hundred acres of farmland in western Illinois adjacent to the Mississippi River. For the Starrs, the flood of '93 was a great catastrophe. They watched in horror as the flood waters moved ever closer to their land. Maybe the rains would let up in time. Maybe the crest of the flood had already been reached and they were safe. Maybe the flood waters would miraculously miss their land. Such were their hopes. This land was their livelihood. This land was their life. "Please God, please!" they cried out in prayer, "spare the land." But the land was not spared. The waters lapped around the edges at first. Then the torrent broke loose. Every acre was under water. There would be no crops this year. There would be an erosion of their soil to devastate future years as well. The Starrs were devastated.

But the worst was yet to come. Their concern had been with their land and livelihood. Now the waters moved in toward their home. Grandpa Starr had had the foresight to build the land up around the house just in case the river would ever spill forth. The Starrs hadn't even thought to worry about the house. As the waters rose relentlessly, however, the house became a grave concern. Maybe one could survive without one's land but how in the world could one survive without one's home? Their prayers now turned to their home. They prayed to God to spare their home. "Spare our home, Lord," they pleaded. "It's all we have." But it was not to be. The raging river inundated their home as well. The basement filled with water. But that was not the end of it. Water rose up four feet high on the main floor of the two-story house.

At first Tom and Donna Starr thought they could ride out the flood safe in their home. They soon realized, however, that their lives would be endangered if they tried to wait out the flood in their house. They would have to abandon everything they held dear. Then another shock wave hit them. Could they get out? Would the pick-up make it through? Were the roads open? Their prayers turned personal. "Spare our lives, dear Lord," they prayed. "Just help us get out of here alive."

The Starrs did get out alive. Their lives were spared. The land was good as gone. So was their house. "We've got nothing left," Tom said to Donna after they finally reached shelter. Donna was silent for a moment. She looked at Tom with tears in her eyes and whispered, "We've got each other. We've got our love." It was Tom's turn to be silent. Finally he spoke, "We've got God's love too."

Tom and Donna Starr agreed that day. On the one hand they had lost just about all their earthly treasures. But they had love. They had their love for each other and their family. They had the love of God. The flood hadn't even touched the greatest treasure of all.

Epiphany 5
Luke 5:1-11

How The Mighty Have Fallen!

Narrative Analogy: *Luke 9:18-20, 28-36; 22:31-62*

"How the mighty have fallen." King David of old once spoke those words concerning the death of King Saul. "How the mighty have fallen." These words have transcended the Bible and become the language of popular culture. A newspaper report a few years ago on some pastors who had fallen from grace used this biblical passage as its headline. The article was about two well-known television preachers — Jimmy Swaggart and Jim Bakker — whose sins had been publicly exposed. "How the mighty have fallen" the newspaper headline gloated!

Jimmy Swaggart is an interesting case in point. *Newsweek* magazine once carried an article that featured this highly talented preacher. The article quoted one man as saying that Jimmy Swaggart was one of the most entertaining people on television in any field. The man didn't believe what Swaggart preached but he was dazzled by his entertainment and communication skills. "How the mighty have fallen!"

Swaggart's sin seemed to be his fascination with pornography. One who knew him well over the years said: "His weakness for pornography finally beat him. He's fasted and prayed many times to overcome this weakness." Swaggart's weakness for pornography often led him to Louisiana brothels. It doesn't appear to be the case that Swaggart had sex with these women. He just asked them to pose for him in some suggestive ways. One night as he was leaving a brothel, however, someone who was out to expose him took some pictures. The pictures undid him. Scandal raged. Swaggart faced his congregation with tears running down his cheeks and remorse in his heart.

The response to Swaggart's fall was highly judgmental. People judged Swaggart harshly because he had been so judgmental in his preaching. In his judgments he came down on all sorts and varieties of people, including Christian people. Of the ministry of Jim Bakker, for example, Swaggart had said: "He's a cancer on the body of Christ that needs to be excised." Swaggart's preaching was judgmental indeed.

Swaggart was also judged harshly because of the peculiar nature of his message. Swaggart's message went beyond the proclamation of Jesus Christ to be a message fundamentally about the holiness work of the Holy Spirit. He proclaimed over and over again that through the work of the Holy Spirit in our lives we can overcome all sin. Thus he judged sinners. Thus he invited sinners to be filled with the Holy Spirit in order to overcome all sin. Victory over sin would belong to all those who did business with the Holy Spirit. What are we to think of this promise in light of Swaggart's own dark side? It's no wonder that some people relished the chance to defrock Swaggart in public. The mighty had fallen indeed.

Jimmy Swaggart is back in his pulpit today. Hopefully he is a much wiser man than he was before. A hint of wisdom is evident in some of the things he says. For example, he says now: "I have seen that the gospel is perfect but its messengers are not." Jimmy Swaggart just might be ready to start his ministry from the same base that Peter began his ministry. "Depart from me, for I am a sinful man, O Lord." Ministry always begins in confession!

Epiphany 6
Luke 6:17-26

With Fire In His Eyes

Narrative Analogy: *Luke 1:51-53; 4:18; 12:13-31; 16:1-15; 16:19-31; 18:18-30; 19:1-10*

There was fire in his eyes as Dr. Yacob spoke. Dr. Yacob is from the northernmost part of ancient Ethiopia. This northern area of Ethiopia has recently become a nation of its own, the nation of Eritrea. Dr. Yacob was born and raised in Asmara, the capital of Eritrea. Early on in his life he had a fire in his eyes for the gospel message of Jesus Christ. In his school days he was already an evangelist telling other students about Jesus. He fought with school authorities in order to get a place on the school grounds where the students might meet for Bible study and prayer.

After high school Dr. Yacob attended the Lutheran seminary in Addis Ababa, Ethiopia. He was a dilligent student. He eventually received a scholarship to study abroad and received his Ph.D. in Old Testament studies. In 1978 Dr. Yacob was elected to be the general secretary of the Evangelical Lutheran Church of Eritrea. These were difficult times. Eritrea was fighting a full scale civil war with Ethiopia. The nation was paralyzed. The resources for life — things like food, water, firewood, gas and electricity — were very scarce. People lived on the edge of desperate poverty. People lived on the edge of death.

In the midst of this poverty, war and destruction Dr. Yacob was determined to rebuild many of the church buildings that had been destroyed. The churches were very well attended in these years. "Every Sunday is like Christmas," Dr. Yacob once said. With the help of overseas partners many of the churches in Eritrea were rebuilt in the midst of ruin. Many questioned Dr. Yacob's choice of church building in this desperate situation. "Building a building is a sign of hope," he maintained with fire in his eyes. "We trust God to be Lord of Life in the midst of death. The buildings were like miracles for us. Jeremiah bought a field at Anathoth just when he thought the land was to be taken away by destruction. His action was a sign of hope for the future. Our buildings are a sign of hope for our future. All could see that in the midst of death, the church was alive."

Dr. Yacob works in France now in the Department of Ecumenical Research for the Lutheran World Federation. This is a leader tested by life. This is a leader who has lived through the hell of war and poverty. Now he travels the whole world over. In far too many places he sees the same kind of conditions that he once saw in Eritrea. Poverty stalks the earth in a million guises. Poverty has churned up his insides. He has simply seen too much suffering.

Speaking to a group of Lutheran missionaries not long ago Dr. Yacob spoke with the accustomed fire in his eyes. "These conditions around the world must stop," he exploded. "I've talked with Lutheran leaders in churches around the world where poverty reigns. We decry the working of the economic systems of our world today. We decry the economic injustice that we see everywhere. We decry a world where some live in magnificent luxury while the world's billions starve to death. This has to stop! We are ready to propose that world Lutheranism adopt it as a basic confession of being a Christian that economic systems which create injustice and inequity must be rejected."

Exchanging A Smile

He smiled when we would have expected him to cry. He smiled when we expected him to hate. He smiled when we expected him to revile. Tshenuwani Simon Farisani is a leader in one of the churches in South Africa. As a leader he felt it his duty to take a stand against the official government policy of *apartheid*. *Apartheid* means apartness. It's about keeping the races totally apart and separate from each other. Fortunately, the policy of *apartheid* has just recently been abandoned in South Africa. The abandonment of this policy, however, came only after years of immense suffering by the peoples of color in South Africa.

Because he stood against *apartheid*, Rev. Farisani was imprisoned many times. He was arrested first in 1976. Police surrounded his house. First his feelings were that he felt himself to be totally outside of the protection of God. Indescribable fear filled his being. The police accused him of being a communist and a terrorist. Farisani was arrested and commandeered to a prison 1,000 kilometers from his home. Said Farisani: "My world came to an end. No company, no freedom of movement, no say about food ... I was a creature without rights, a non-being."

And he was tortured. Endlessly. He was taken to yet another prison and handcuffed and leg-ironed. He remembers only punches and kicks. His hair was pulled out. His beard was uprooted. He was thrown to the floor then commanded to stand. He was thrown to the floor again and on and on it went, the thunders of the blows punctuating his groaning. Then they dangled his body upside down out of a window. "Answer us or we will let you fall to the ground and scatter your

39

brains everywhere,'' his torturers growled. "We'll tell the world that you jumped!''

In subsequent tortures over the years Farisani experienced electric shock and more beatings. He cried out to God in prayer and God finally sent what seemed to be angels to relieve him. In fact, he has said, God sent so many angels to comfort him that he urged God to send some of them to his cellmates.

God was with Rev. Farisani. So in the midst of this indescribable suffering he could sing, "I will walk tall in Jesus' name. Food with worms, I will eat tall. My wife, my children, congregations away, I will walk tall in Jesus' name. Wounds all over, I will walk tall in Jesus' name. Pangs of prison, I walk tall in Jesus' name. Tall fences around, I walk taller in Jesus' name!''

Rev. Farisani should have grown to hate these bloody torturers. But he did not. Instead, he began to pray for them. Only after he had prayed for them, he has said, did he realize how much his guards and torturers needed daily, serious-minded intercessions. To all to whom he has told his story he has asked for prayers of intercession for the security police.

And one day in prison he smiled. He exchanged a simple smile with one of his torturers in order to sow a small seed of love in a world of hatred and division. He smiled when he would have been expected to hate. He smiled when he would have been expected to revile. God had given him such peace in the midst of hate that he could dare even to exchange a smile. These are the smiles that change the world.

Glory of God shining through Him.

good

The Glory And The Pain

Narrative Analogy: *Luke 3:21-22; Luke 9:18-27; Luke 24:26, 44-49*

His given name was Leslie Leonard but everyone just called him "Pete." Pete was the son of very devout parents. They saw to it that the seeds of faith were planted in him. They were there to nourish the seeds along. Once he got out on his own in life, however, it appeared that the seeds of faith had not taken very deep root in Pete's soul. He sowed wild oats instead. He appeared to have left behind him the faith of his parents.

Early on life went well for Pete. He married, had a son, was involved with a number of businesses. He had some successes in his life. What was most successful about him was his personality. Pete was a charmer. He had a ready smile for all whom he encountered. People who were swept into his life's orbit couldn't help but like him. He was just that kind of guy.

As the years passed by things were not easy for Pete. His marriage failed him. His only son failed him as well. And then the greatest tragedy of all occurred. His health failed him. In his early 40s he was stricken with multiple sclerosis. He was totally blind and paralyzed from the neck down. Eventually he got back the use of his upper body though his eyes and his legs never recovered. After some years one of his legs had to be amputated. Suffering covered Pete's life like a blanket.

Blind and crippled Pete had every earthly reason to be bitter over his state in life. He had every earthly reason to complain. He had every earthly reason to hate life and God. But he didn't. Miraculously, as his suffering increased, his faith increased as well. He hinted at times that there in his hospital

41

bed, in the first days of his MS, God had been revealed to him in a special way. Whatever the reason, Pete was a new man. The faith planted by his parents blossomed at last!

People often went to visit Pete. After a visit to him a man said of his experience, "I went to cheer him up and it was he who cheered me up. It's always like that with him."

His pastor spoke similar words about Pete. "I don't go to call on Pete in order to minister to him," they would often say. "I go to call on Pete when I need someone to talk to; when I need someone to minister to me. I take my problems to him. In his blindness he sees more than just about anyone I know."

As long as he was able, Pete was in church every Sunday. There was a space reserved for him in the last row where his wheelchair would easily fit. Through the cajoling of his pastors Pete also served many terms on the church council. He was one of the leaders of his congregation. His common sense and his faith tested-by-fire helped him to pierce to the core of many of the issues that faced the congregation. He was blind but he could see things that most people could never see. He was immobile of body but mobile of mind and thought.

When Pete died the whole congregation mourned. On a bitter winter day the church was full for his funeral. The pastor put into words that day what most of them had thought. "We saw in him the glory of God," the pastor said, "the glory of God shining through the depths of human suffering. Thanks be to God."

True Repentance

"Today we're going to talk about Lent," Tanya announced at the beginning of the adult class she had been teaching for more than 20 years. "It dawned on me the other day that in all the years I've been teaching this class we've never talked about Lent." The class members seemed to agree and Tanya Washington began her Lenten discussions by giving the class members some background on the history of Lent. Then she asked her class how they thought about Lent.

"Mostly I think of Lent as a time to give up something, make some kind of sacrifice," said Jawan Black. "I've just about run out of things to give up on though. Don't know what I'll give up this year."

Shamal Pippen saw Lent from a different angle. "I think Lent is about repentance," he said. "It's a time to rethink your life before God and dedicate yourself anew to be about the will of God. I know I can do better with my life. Lent's good for me that way. It gets me into thinking about what I can do to better myself in the eyes of God and in the eyes of others."

"How do the rest of you feel about that?" Tanya Washington asked.

"I think Shamal's got it about right," replied another member. "Lent is about repentance all right. I know I can do a lot better with my life, too."

"What is true repentance?" Ms. Washington asked of them all.

"It's feeling sorry for your sins," said one. "It's feeling sorry for your sins plus a vow of improvement. I can do better. That's the heart of repentance."

As the class discussed the matter of true repentance they came to general agreement. Repentance consists of at least two acts. First, it's feeling sorry for what you've done wrong. Second, it's a promise that you can and will do better in the future.

Tanya Washington let the class mull over their consensus for a few moments. Then she announced rather sternly, "Well, I for one disagree totally with this kind of thinking about repentance. I've been repenting like that all of my life but it never seems to do me any good. I don't think it's done all of you much good either. Here we all say that each year in Lent we feel sorry for our sins and promise that we can and will do better but who does any better? I don't, for one.

"It seems to me that my promises are just like so much straw in the wind. I say I can and will do better but I don't. That's made me think about this repentance business in a new way. What's the point of promising we can do better all the time when we don't do it anyway? This year I decided that I'm not going to promise that I can do better. This year I'm going to confess to God that *I can't* do any better. I've said, 'I can,' for years but I don't. So why not just tell God, 'I can't.' I can't do better Lord. That's why I come to you. I don't have the power to remake myself but you have the power to remake me as a new person.

"This year in Lent I'm just going to say to God, 'I can't.' I'm going to ask God to do for me what I can't do for myself. I think that's what true repentance is all about. To 'return the Lord with all your heart,' means to turn away from running my life under my own power and offering my life to the power of God."

A Man Who Would Be God

Narrative Analogy: *Luke 3:21-22, 23-38; Luke 4:16-21; Luke 9:28-36*

It was to be his first trip back to China. He was born in China to missionary parents in the 1930s. When his parents had to flee China and return to the States because of the Second World War, however, Tom Stone came with them. And he had never been back; never seen the land of his birth — until his journey in the 1990s. As the plane landed in Beijing his heart began to pound. What would it be like? Would he remember anything? What would he discover about himself in this land of his birth?

Tom Stone took in China like a breath of fresh air. He loved so very much of what it was. The Great Wall. China's bustling cities. The gentle people. The vast landscape. Wonderful! Breathtaking! Exciting! How good it was to be home again. He found China much to his liking except for one thing — one thing that he had not expected to find. He thought the great Chairman Mao Tse-tung was dead and gone. Not so. It seemed like he ran into the image of the Chairman at every turn.

Tom knew that Chairman Mao had written *The Little Red Book* as a kind of "bible" of his thoughts. Tom assumed that *The Little Red Book* was a thing of the past, tucked away with memories of the Chairman. But it was not so. *The Little Red Book* was for sale everywhere. The Chairman's "bible" functioned like the "bible" for many Chinese people.

If it wasn't *The Little Red Book* that reminded Tom Stone of the Chairman there were plenty of other reminders. Aluminum buttons with Mao's picture on it were abundantly evident. He saw them everywhere on people's clothing. People wore them proudly as a way to venerate their great ancestor. "Was this just nostalgia?" Tom wondered, "or are these people looking to Mao as a kind of god?"

Once he had become aware of the presence of Mao, Tom Stone found him everywhere. Posters and portraits of the Chairman were omnipresent. "Why do you hang his picture like that?" Tom asked one day. "Mao's picture helps to ward off evil spirits," he was told. Elsewhere Tom saw a woman trudging up the streets caressing a tiny bronze statue of Mao. "Mao made us proud of China," the woman said to Tom. "Our leaders now dishonor his name."

Tom Stone had discovered that for millions and millions of Chinese citizens Mao Tse-tung still lives and is believed to exercise supernatural powers on behalf of his people. Perhaps the greatest sign of all this was the way in which Mao had become the "St. Christopher" of China. Nearly every taxi he entered and every truck that he saw carrying goods for the life blood of modern day China, prominently displayed a portrait of Chairman Mao. His face dangled from rear view mirrors or was plastered on the dash board of their vehicles. Mao Tse-tung was, indeed, respected and venerated as a godlike man.

Tom Stone had read much on China. He had read much on Mao Tse-tung. He knew that Chairman Mao sought to portray himself to his people as one larger than life. Mao was a man who was sorely tempted to reach for the stars. He was a mortal who reached for immortality. He was a man who would be god. Millions of Chinese people today firmly believe that Mao was, indeed, a man who would be god.

46

A Mother's Tears

Narrative Analogy: *Luke 9:51ff; 19:28-44; 21:20-24; 23:27-31; 24:44-53*

Gertrude Schmidt loved being a mother. She truly felt that motherhood was her one true vocation in life. Gertrude's devotion to her calling came most clearly to light after her husband, Horst, died. Gertrude and Horst had had three children of their own. Peter was 12, Monica was ten and Sebastian was six when their father died. Gertrude threw herself into the task of mothering more than ever before.

It was difficult, of course, for Gertrude Schmidt to support her family now that Horst was gone. There was a small pension and social security but that was barely enough to keep the family afloat! Gertrude pondered her situation. She came up with a splendid idea! If she would take in foster children for the state she would be given a stipend for raising them. This was the best of all worlds she thought. She could go on being what she wanted to be: a mother. And, she would make additional money in the process.

It wasn't easy for Gertrude Schmidt to convince the social agency that she ought to be allowed to raise foster children. Normally such children were only assigned to homes with two parents. But Gertrude persisted. This one time, therefore, the agency made an exception. They began to assign foster children to the care of Gertrude Schmidt.

Gertrude was overjoyed at this turn of events. She plunged into motherhood with more gusto than ever. She loved her own children. She loved the foster children who were assigned to her. She spoke of them all tenderly referring to them often as, "my flock."

Over the years, however Gertrude Schmidt's joy at being a mother turned into grief. The first foster child she took in was a 15-year-old boy named Gary. Gary had been in and out of many foster homes leaving much trouble in his wake. Gertrude was undeterred. She would take Gary in and love him into manhood. But it didn't work. Gary ran with a rough crowd. One night he had been with some boys who were drinking. There was an automobile accident. Gary was killed. And Gertrude wept.

Her own son, Peter, had really taken to Gary. He, too, was filled with grief over Gary's accidental death. In his grief Peter turned sullen. He spoke hardly a word. And then one day, Peter was gone. No note, no words of farewell, simply gone. Grief had driven him to the chase. And Gertrude wept.

A second foster child, a girl named Cynthia, came to live under the loving care and protection of Gertrude Schmidt. Cynthia had originally come from a very wealthy home. She was quite spoiled. It was hard for her to take the near poverty conditions that reigned at Gertrude Schmidt's place. She wanted so many things. She wanted them so badly that she began to steal them. Cynthia was caught shoplifting several times. The judge, listening to Gertrude's loving pleas, tried to be lenient. Leniency did not work, however, and Cynthia was finally put in juvenile detention.

Once again, Gertrude wept. Her heart was broken. She had given all of the love she could muster to her "flock." If only she could just gather them all up in her arms and love them. But her love was spurned. And Gertrude wept. It's all she knew how to do. Gertrude wept.

Lent 3
Luke 13:1-9

A Modern Day Job

American culture is a culture of fixing blame — fixing blame on others. Whenever the President of our land slips a bit the media ask, "Why? Who is to blame?" When our favorite sports team loses, the question is asked, "Why? Who is to blame?" And on and on it goes. We are anxious to fix the blame somewhere. This "blame" culture may nowhere be so clearly seen as in the mountain of court cases brought in our land. It's getting to the point that when anything wrong happens to anyone the first thought is to go to court in order to assign the blame to someone else.

There lives a man whose name is J. B. J. B. is a lot like an Old Testament character named Job. J. B. protests his innocence when anything goes wrong. His method of choice for assigning blame is a lawsuit. J. B. is a rugged, athletic man. He is very proud of his body. He boasts of his feats of strength. So when the local YMCA advertised a "Refrigerator Race" J. B. signed up immediately. In this kind of race a refrigerator is strapped to your back. The one who can move ten yards the most quickly with a refrigerator on his back wins the race. This was just the kind of stuff that J. B. loved. He strapped on the refrigerator and away he went. And then the strap broke. Down came J. B., refrigerator, and all. His back was hurt to be sure. But his pride was hurt more than his back.

"Who is to blame?" J. B. thought. His answer: The company that made the strap. What to do? He thought it over and said, "I'll sue." He sued the strap company for one million dollars. They were to blame. He was innocent. He sued and he won! The blame was not his!

On another occasion J. B.'s equally physical son crashed the seat of a swing into the head of another young man. There was brain damage to the other boy. What was more important to J. B., however, was the damage to his own reputation. "Who is to blame?" J. B. thought. His answer: The company that made the wooden swing seat. What to do? He thought it over and he said, "I'll sue." He sued the company that made the swing seat for making a seat that could hurt someone. They were to blame. He was innocent. He sued and he won! Two million dollars this time! The blame was not his!

J. B. lived in suburbia. He took pride in his house and his yard. One day while he was out working in his yard he noticed that his neighbor, Mike, was also working on his yard. They each paused for a bit in their work and talked over the hedge. They began discussing the fact that the hedge between them needed trimming. Since Mike was standing with his lawn mower, J. B. suggested that they hold the lawn mower up by its four wheels, two men on each side of the hedge, and use the lawn mower as a hedge clipper. Great idea! And it worked — for a while. Then J. B. stepped into a hole, lost his balance and down he went with the mower on top of him. His hand was badly cut.

As always, J. B.'s first thought was, "Who is to blame?" It just couldn't be his fault. It couldn't be his stupidity. The last place he would think of looking to assign blame was to himself. Who is to blame? The lawn mower company, of course. Nowhere in their directions did they indicate that this machine should not be used as a hedge clipper. What to do? He thought it over and he said, "I'll sue." And sue he did. The lawn mower company was to blame. The court agreed. He was innocent. The blame was not his!

P.S. The legal facts in this parable are true!

Lent 4
Luke 15:1-3, 11b-32

The Lost Is Found

It was the biggest tragedy in Pastor Dave's life. Kathy, his daughter, had always been a problem child. There were medical problems. There were behavioral problems. Life was not easy with this daughter. And then one day — when she was 23 years old — Kathy simply disappeared. She was gone and no one could find her.

Weeks went by. Pastor Dave was racked with worry. Months went by. Pastor Dave was sure that she must be dead by now. What chance did she have in the world all alone? She needed her medicine. She needed care. Years went by. Pastor Dave felt like he had been through a wringer. He had prayed more than he had prayed in his whole life. He tried to turn the matter over to God. He tried to have this burden lifted from his shoulders. Nothing worked. Kathy's disappearance left a pit in his stomach and a grief in his heart. It was awful.

And then one day, ten years after Kathy had disappeared, the telephone rang at Pastor Dave's house. It was the State Mental Hospital in another part of the state. "We are making an inquiry here," the voice on the line said rather matter-of-factly. "We have a Jane Doe in our care. We have no idea who she is. She has no idea who she is. But we have her Social Security number and we believe her name is Kathy. She thinks she remembers her parents' names. We've cross-checked the records in our state and you folks seem to fit the information we have. Do you have a missing daughter?"

Pastor Dave was speechless. He couldn't believe what he was hearing. Ten long years! Could it really be that his daughter, now 33, was still alive? Had God heard their prayers? "Well, yes," he finally answered, "we do have a missing daughter named Kathy." As they spoke further on the phone Pastor Dave was quite sure that it was, indeed, his Kathy who had been found. Arrangements were made for Dave and his wife to come to the hospital as quickly as possible in order to identify Kathy. They made the trip in a state of excited anticipation. And it was true! It really was Kathy. The lost had been found.

Having found his daughter Pastor Dave and his wife could instruct the nurses on her medical history. Kathy seemed to respond quite well. It wasn't long before the hospital was ready to release her. Pastor Dave drove across the state once again for the last time since Kathy was found. He could still hardly believe that after ten lost years he was actually going to pick up his daughter. But it was true. Pastor Dave arrived at Kathy's room and helped her pack her few things. He carried them out to the car. After signing the proper release papers Pastor Dave and Kathy were free to go. They got in the car for what was to be a joyous ride home.

As the car pulled out of the hospital grounds no words were exchanged between father and daughter. The only sound was the sound of sniffles as tears flowed down both faces. Finally, a couple of miles down the road, Kathy spoke. "It's kind of like the prodigal son isn't it, Dad? Except that I'm a girl."

"That's exactly what it's like," said Pastor Dave choking back his tears. "And you remember the joy with which the father welcomed his son home? Well that's just how I feel today. Welcome home, Kathy."

A New Thing

"I'm telling you it's just not possible that he is the Messiah. If anything he's an imposter. No one should be saying and doing the kinds of things he says and does. It's blasphemy. The man should be killed."

Those were Eliezer's heartfelt convictions. Eliezer and his friend, Amos, were teachers of the law in the days that Jesus walked this earth. They were terribly puzzled by the appearance of this Jesus. Eliezer would have none of Jesus' ministry or of his teaching. He was convinced that whatever else Jesus was, the verdict was in and he most certainly was not the promised Messiah. Amos, on the other hand, wasn't so sure. He didn't know just what to think of this carpenter's son from Nazareth.

"Oh, come on, Amos," Eliezer said to him one day. "You were there when we caught him going through the grainfields on the sabbath to feed himself and his disciples. Do you actually believe that the Messiah would break our religious laws? Be serious. He's an imposter I tell you."

"And that's not all." Eliezer was warming to his topic now. His voice raised. "He also healed that man with the withered hand on the sabbath day," he bellowed at Amos. "That's work on the sabbath day. That's also against our laws. I don't know what we're going to do with this man but we've got to put a stop to him pretty quickly or he is going to mislead our people. The man has got to be stopped. He violates traditions that have been passed on to us for generations. He is not true to our past. Such a one simply cannot be the Messiah."

Amos didn't respond to Eliezer's charge. He honestly didn't know just what to say. It was surely true that Jesus was shattering old religious traditions. But what did that mean?

Eliezer never let up in seeking to persuade his friend Amos of the danger of this man who brought so much novelty to their land. "Did you hear what he did at Joab's house?" he demanded of Amos one day. "A prostitute got into the house somehow and washed his feet with her tears and anointed them with ointment. As Joab said, 'If Jesus was really the Messiah he would have known what kind of woman this was and cast her out of the house.' Whoever heard of a Messiah who lets himself be cleansed by sinners? The very idea violates everything we hold dear."

Amos kept quiet. He knew Eliezer's words were true. Jesus certainly was upsetting their religious fruitbasket. Still, Amos couldn't simply condemn Jesus. Eliezer kept the pressure on. "Look at who he associates with," Eliezer screamed at him one day. "He receives sinners and eats with them. Table fellowship is sacred, Amos. You only eat with those with whom you have the deepest ties of friendship. I say, 'If he eats with sinners, he is a sinner.' I challenge you to find one word in scripture that suggests that our long-awaited Messiah is to be in fellowship with sinners. The truth is that the Messiah comes for the faithful, comes for the law abiding, comes for those who have held fast the traditions of the past."

And Amos finally spoke. He said one word, "Isaiah."

"What do you mean, Isaiah?" Eliezer shot back.

"Maybe it's as Isaiah wrote," Amos said. " 'Do not remember the former things, or consider the things of old. I am about to do a new thing ...' "

A Promise On The Way To Fulfillment

Narrative Analogy: *Luke 2:1-14; 9:51 et al; 13:31-35; 19:41-44*

It had been the night of his life. He would never forget it as long as he lived. Aaron was a shepherd who lived and worked near Bethlehem in days long ago. On that greatest night of all he had been just a young boy getting his first taste of a shepherd's way of life. Everybody had told him that a shepherd's life would be boring. Well, it wasn't boring that night! A frenzy of excitement was in the air.

There they were, himself, his dad and his big brother. The excitement stirred their very being. An angel appeared to them in the sky. God's glory shone all around them. It was scary at first. They were all tempted to just leave the sheep and run. What was this anyway, the end of the world? But the angel reassured them. "Do not be afraid," the angel had said. That calmed their hearts and they listened to the angel's words that God's Messiah would be born in Bethlehem. A baby wrapped in diapers would be the sign.

As Aaron and the other men began to ponder what these words might mean the heavens filled with a multitude of the heavenly host. "Glory to God in the highest," they sang, "and on earth, peace among those whom God favors." When the heavenly chorus was finished, Aaron and the shepherds headed for Bethlehem. They found the baby in diapers all right. Aaron didn't know what to think. He was both dazzled and confused. How in the world, he wondered to himself, is this tiny baby going to bring peace on earth? In the mind of a young boy the whole thing just didn't add up.

Years passed and nothing came of this whole event. Aaron was middle-aged by now and living in Jerusalem. He heard some stories, some rumors, about Jesus of Nazareth. Some folks thought this Jesus just might be the Messiah who would bring peace on earth. Angels and glory and a heavenly chorus tend to fade out over the years, however. The whole thing still seemed a bit improbable to Aaron the Shepherd.

Then one sabbath day Aaron heard the sound of many voices. He ran quickly toward the source of the sound. Very slowly his eyes began to make out a multitude of people moving toward the city. Aaron watched with interest as the seemingly jubilant crowd moved his way. The attention of the crowd was fixed upon a man riding upon a colt. He was certain that the man was Jesus. The baby in diapers had grown up! People were throwing their garments on the ground making a kind of road-of-cloth for the man and his colt. Aaron hadn't felt such excitement in the air since the night the angels appeared to him near Bethlehem some 30 odd years ago.

The pulsing crowd came closer now. They shouted out words of praise to Jesus. "Blessed is the king who comes in the name of the Lord!" he heard them shout. It was the next line of their chant, however, that really captured his attention and lifted him back in time to the night on those Bethlehem hills. "Peace in heaven, and glory in the highest heaven!" the crowd shouted. That's almost exactly the same song that the angels sang over the hills of Bethlehem, Aaron thought in some excitement. Maybe the words of the angels' promise were coming to fulfillment at last. Maybe this baby-in-diapers-carpenter's-son would make it happen.

Easter Day
Luke 24:1-12

A Shroud Unto Life

Who will ever forget those first pictures? There were pictures of starving men and starving women and starving children. These pictures stunned the world when they first hit our television screens. Pictures of Ethiopia. Pictures of an incredible famine. Millions of lives were at risk. And the world hardly knew about it until we saw the pictures.

It was the pictures of the starving children that probably carried the most power. Babies sucking desperately at mother's empty breast, sucking for their life. Large brown eyes filled with tears and flies and fear. Distended stomachs. Bodies unimaginably lean. Innocent young lives were being snuffed out. The world shook its head in disbelief.

The pictures, of course, motivated the world to action. Relief agencies from all over the world began to pour into Ethiopia. Christian organizations from our country also rushed to the scene of the disaster. Kathleen O'Meara was sent to Ethiopia on behalf of her church. Kathleen looked forward to the challenge. She had offered her life to her church for just such an occasion and now she would have a chance for service to humankind that would call forth her best gifts of serving.

When Ms. O'Meara arrived in Ethiopia, however, she was nearly overwhelmed by the devastating power of the famine. She was assigned to work in a feeding station in the northern part of Ethiopia. She went north with a convoy of trucks bearing sack upon sack upon sack of food. After two days of arduous travel the caravan finally arrived at its destination. Kathleen had seen many people along the roadside on the way north begging for food. At the feeding station, however, starving people were just about all she saw. It seemed that for as far as her eye could see she saw nothing but starving, dying people. There were faint sounds from the youngest children. There were wails of despair from the lips of many of the women. There was an utter look of resignation and defeat in the eyes of men whose bodies were long and gaunt.

Now there was work to be done. Kathleen was assigned to help distribute the many sacks of food that had been brought by the convoy. Sacks! Night and day that's all she would think of; all she could do. She saw those sacks in her troubled sleep each night. Sacks of food. Sacks that could bring life. Sacks were her mission and her hope.

For Kathleen it was a daily round with the life-giving sacks of food. She came to see those sacks in her mind as a kind of symbol of hope in the midst of the devastation. And then one day her eyes caught sight of an event that shattered her vision of the sacks as life-giving agents. That day she saw several hundred dead Ethiopians being carried to their graves in a funeral shroud. To her dismay the empty food sacks had now been filled with dead bodies. Sacks of life had become shrouds of death.

The bitter irony of it all was almost too much for Ms. O'Meara. Sacks of life had become shrouds of death. She pondered deeply on this awful turn of events. "What the world needs," she mused to herself, "is for someone wrapped in the shrouds of death to bring new life and hope to the world." Sacks of life had become shrouds of death. What if a shroud of death became a garment of life? Would anyone believe such a story? Or would the world pass it off as just an idle tale?

Easter 2
John 20:19-31 *Believing to Seeing*

"This Is My Body"

Tommy Russo tried and tried to go to church with his wife. Sophia Russo was the one who had been brought up in the church. Her parents had been very devout Christian people. With Tommy's parents it was completely different. They didn't attend church and they didn't make their kids attend either. At this point in their marriage, therefore, Tommy and Sophia Russo faced a real dilemma. Tommy had promised he'd give church a try. And he did. But the whole thing left him sort of cold. He just couldn't buy it all. There was just too much there that was unbelievable!

Tommy tried talking to Sophia about it one Sunday after they had been to church. "Can't we find some kind of compromise on this religion thing?" Tommy asked. But Sophia would have none of it. Her Christian faith meant the world to her. She was not about to compromise. She was not about to give up her faith practices. "You promised," she said to Tommy. "You said you would give it a try."

"But I have tried," Tommy replied. "How long do I have to go on with this anyway? I've been to church with you just about every Sunday for this whole first year of our marriage. Isn't that trying? What more do you want from me? Enough is enough. There's just too much about church and all that I just can't believe."

"What *can* you believe about it all?" Sophia asked.

"Jesus," Tommy blurted out after a few moments of silence. "I like Jesus. He makes a lot of sense to me at times. There's some very good advice about life in his teachings. But to buy into Jesus I've got to buy into too much other stuff that is not helpful at all. In fact, it just confuses the issue.

Take this Virgin Mary business, for example. I mean, come on! Get serious. Stuff like that just doesn't happen. And what's the use of it anyway? Does it make Jesus any better than he already is? I don't think so. And then there's the miracles and the final miracle: 'he was raised from the dead.' I feel the same way about that as I do about his birth. So what? Jesus was a great man, a great teacher. I don't need all this miracle business. I honestly doubt that it really happened that way. Maybe the disciples just made it up for all we know."

At the end of their discussion, however, Tommy agreed to keep his promise and go with her on Sundays for a few more months. One Sunday the gospel reading caught him up short. It was about Thomas. That was his name. Thomas had doubts. So did he. He liked what Thomas had to say about Jesus being raised from the dead. "Unless I see the mark of the nails in his hands, and put my finger in the mark of the nails and my hand in his side, I will not believe." Tommy Russo couldn't have put it better himself. "If only I could see his body," he thought to himself. "If only I could touch his body. That's the way we Thomas people are."

Tommy's mind got fixed on the Bible's doubting Thomas. That's all he could think about for the rest of the service. That's what he thought about when he and Sophia went up for communion. "If only I could see his body. If I only could touch his body." And then Tommy's reverie was interrupted by the pastor's words. The words jolted his consciousness. It was just a simple word. "This is my body given for you."

Easter 3
Acts 9:1-6 (7-20) : *Uncertainty about Decisions*

When The Light From Heaven Does Not Flash

Dawn Hetland didn't move a muscle. The worship service was over. The choir had filed out. The pastor was at the back door greeting the worshippers. The pews were quickly becoming empty. But Dawn did not move. She sat silently, her hands folded, her head bowed in prayer.

Bridget Glass was a life-long friend of Dawn Hetland. As she was leaving the sanctuary that Sunday morning she happened to see her friend Dawn with her head bowed low. Bridget thought something must be wrong. She went quickly to Dawn's side, tapped her on the shoulder, and asked if everything was all right. "Oh, yeah, sure," Dawn replied, orienting herself once again to her surroundings. "I was just praying. I've got an important decision to make and I need all the help and guidance I can get."

"What decision is that?" Bridget asked.

"About my future, Bridget. You know that I've just finished medical school. That's been my goal for any number of years now. So I've finished. So what? What do I do now? I never thought this would all seem so hard and complicated. I've got an offer to join a team of physicians in Tampa, Florida. But I've also been invited to do a residency program in Internal Medicine. I'm really torn between these two offers. All I've ever wanted to do was to be a doctor as a way of living out my Christian faith. Both of these offers open up an opportunity for me to serve God. But which one should I take? What does God want me to do with my life? That's the question I can't answer."

"And that's what you've been sitting here praying for?" Bridget asked.

61

"Yes," Dawn answered. "I really don't know what to do. So I pray. I don't think I've ever prayed for anything so much in my whole life. But I'm not getting any answers. God seems to be very silent!"

"Have you asked for advice from people you trust?" Bridget asked. Dawn nodded her head in assent. "Have you made a list of all the positives and negatives with these two possibilities?" Bridget inquired further. Dawn nodded for a second time. "I don't know what else you can do then," Bridget said in a comforting voice. "You've just got to make a bold decision now and get on with your life."

"That's easy for you to say," Dawn shot back. "How can I make a bold decision when I don't even know what to decide. Why can't I see a flash of light in the sky? Why doesn't a still, small voice speak to me?"

"Now you're asking too much," Bridget replied. "Only a handful of people living or dead have received such signs from God. I don't know if you were here a couple of weeks ago when Pastor Hagedorn preached about discerning God's will for our lives. Make a list of the positives and negatives, he said. Talk to people you trust. Take the matter to God in prayer. Then decide with boldness which course to take."

"But what if I choose the wrong thing?" Dawn wondered aloud.

"The status of your life before God does not depend upon making right decisions," Bridget said firmly. "We live our lives under the canopy of God's forgiving love. Our God of grace will walk with you no matter what path you choose. And remember, 'God works all things together for good with those who love God.' Don't worry, Dawn. God will take your decision, whatever it is, and make the best of it."

Easter 4 *"Peace, nor Hatred, Torment Neighbor"*
Revelation 7:9-17

From All Nations, Tribes, Peoples, Languages

Mina lived in Sarajevo, the capital city of Bosnia-Herzegovina. Mina, along with the majority of people in Sarajevo, was a Muslim. Muslims and Croats and Serbs had lived together, side-by-side and in peace in Sarajevo for many years. But no longer! The Serbs had laid siege to Sarajevo. Every Muslim was a target of their violence.

In time Mina became a target of Serbian violence. The nature of the violence was almost unbelievable. Mina's next door neighbors were Serbs. Mina's family and the Serbian neighbors had been friends for a long time. Mina knew the man next door quite well though her contacts with him were rather formal since she was still in high school. One night Mina had to run a family errand which would keep her out after dark. Being out after dark in Sarajevo was a bit like walking through hell. Mina was frightened as she walked toward home that night. She was really startled, therefore, when a man suddenly walked alongside of her. There was still enough light for her to recognize that it was the man next door. She breathed a sigh of relief. The two of them walked on together in tense silence.

Then, all at once, the neighbor grabbed Mina's arm with brutal strength and forced her into a back alley. In the alley, at knife point, he raped her violently. "Now you will have Serb babies," he hissed at her. Rape had become part of the policy of "ethnic cleansing" in Sarajevo! This kind of rape even of one's neighbors sets the atrocities of Sarajevo apart from almost any other form of human inhumanity. It is estimated that 20,000 to 50,000 women were raped in the conflict that tore open the former country of Yugoslavia.

So Mina was a victim of rape. Mina was a victim of "ethnic cleansing." But Mina's nightmare did not end that night. She was taken to a prison camp where Muslim women were systematically raped until they were most certainly pregnant. Once impregnated, they were released.

Mina returned home a totally beaten and shame-filled woman. She was physically ravished and psychologically destroyed. But her plight was not yet over. The men of her own people felt humiliated by what had happened to women like Mina. They felt that such women were a disgrace to their people. She brought shame also upon them. So, one night, the men came for Mina and took her to an abandoned building. She was just one of many women paraded to the building on that evil night. And then the men pronounced a word of condemnation upon the women. "You have brought shame upon our people," the men said. "We, therefore, condemn you to death." Mina didn't have a chance with these men. She was killed by men of her own people — killed probably out of religious conviction — for the disgrace she had brought upon them.

The women in Mina's neighborhood could hardly believe what their ears heard when they were told of Mina's fate. They thought they had seen everything. "When will it stop?" one woman said. "How can one people hate another people so much?" another wondered out loud. "And this hatred between peoples happens all over the world," said still another. "The human race needs a vision," she continued. "We need a vision of peoples who can live together in peace. Only such a vision can ever lift us beyond our bitter and petty hatreds of each other."

Easter 5
Revelation 21:1-6

No More Tears

Can you imagine a four-year-old boy falling to his death from the 53rd floor of a New York City apartment building? Unimaginable as it seems, that is precisely what happened to the son of British rock star, Eric Clapton. Clapton's life was filled with tears of grief as the result of this shocking event. His son's death haunted him so much that he finally wrote a song about it. He called it, "Tears in Heaven." In February of 1993 this song of Clapton's won the Grammy as the "Song of the Year." Mr. Clapton himself won the Grammy as Male Vocalist of the Year. Eric Clapton, however, would have given up all the success of these Grammys in an instant if he could just have had his son back.

Clapton's song begins with these words: "Would you know my name, if I saw you in heaven? Would it be the same, if I saw you in heaven?" Mr. Clapton's separation from his son is real. His son is gone forever. As with others who grieve the loss of loved ones, however, Clapton desperately wants to communicate with him again.

Clapton's song continues. He envisions heaven for a moment. He knows that heaven is a place that he does not belong. That means that he must somehow find the strength to carry on when he knows, "I don't belong here in heaven." The singer gets a glimpse of heaven, a glimpse of hope. But in heaven he does not belong.

Verse two of "Tears in Heaven" returns to the same theme. He wonders if his son would hold his hand if he saw him in heaven? He wonders, further, whether his son would help him stand if he saw him in heaven? Clapton does not know the answers to his questions. He just believes that if he could get a glimpse of his son again his grief might be lightened. In his grief he cries out for some kind of contact with his son. But it is not to be. So, he sings, "I will have to find my own way, because I just can't stay, here in heaven." The burden of grief rests squarely on his shoulders. Heaven is of no help. Heaven is beyond his grasp. His son is beyond his grasp. He'll just have to make do as best he can. He'll have to "find his own way through night and day." Clapton's song is a very sad song! The grief is so real and the hope so illusory. Clapton knows he doesn't belong in heaven for whatever reason. Therefore, he will have to carry his own grief and his grief is a terribly heavy load.

Clapton sings of this heavy load in the next verse of his song. "Time can bring you down," he sings. Time can be devastating when you are locked in grief. Time can bend your knees; it has you "beggin' please." Such is Clapton's plight. He is reduced to begging. Surely he has begged God to give him a reason for his son's death. Why, God, Why? Surely he has begged God to bring his son back again. Surely he has begged God to lighten his load in life. There is a lot of begging going on in the midst of human tears of grief.

Clapton sees one bright ray of hope in the midst of his grief.He is sure that in heaven there are no tears. That's the source of the song's title: "Tears in Heaven." Tears are for the earth. Tears are grief's constant companion. Tears are grief's way of showing us the pit of emptiness that tugs so heavily upon us in our time of loss. Tears are vital to the healing process. Through the ears, however, Clapton sees a vision of a place where tears shall be no more. "There will be no more tears in heaven," he sings. "There will be no more tears in heaven."

Paths Of Desperation

Where do you go when you feel hopeless? Dick learned something about that when he was 13. Dick was raised in a Lutheran Church and age 13 was confirmation time. The climax of the two-year confirmation program was the public examination. At this examination the pastor put his class on public display. With the parents of the confirmands present, the pastor grilled the students with questions about what they had learned in the course of their two-year instruction period. It was quite an ordeal!

Dick wasn't too worried about the public examination. He had prepared well and knew what was expected of him. On the night of the examination he did just fine. He knew the answer to all the questions the pastor asked and answered some of the questions that the other students didn't get right. Dick felt proud of his performance especially with his mother in the audience. Dick loved his mom very much. She was a warm and loving mother who really seemed to understand a teenage boy.

And Dick was right. His mother was proud of him. She told him so as she drove him home from church that night. Dick went to bed feeling pretty darn good about himself. When he woke up the next morning, however, his world turned quickly upside down. His mother was gone. She had hemorrhaged during the night and his dad had taken her to the hospital. When his dad returned from the hospital with the bad news Dick got a real earful. "Your mother started bleeding before I got home from work last night," he said to Dick. "She said she cried out to you in the night and you didn't hear her." Dick's dad was very angry with him. Dick felt terrible about the whole thing. How could he let his mother down like that?

The news from the hospital was grim. The family had known that their mother had had cancer for about a year and now the doctors gave her only six months to live. They had no cure for her ovarian cancer. She would surely die. That's when Dick learned about hopelessness.

Dick's dad was also in shock. And he was angry. He was angry with the doctors who had seemed to give up hope on his wife. Suddenly hopelessness was the order of the day. And where to go with this hopelessness? Dick's parents found a place that offered some hope for cancer treatment. A doctor about an hour's drive away claimed to have a cure for this type of cancer. Before long Dick's mother was housed with that doctor in the far away town. Dick made the drive with his father to see his mother quite often. This trip was this family's only hope. They knew of nowhere else to go with their hopelessness. They had to drive an hour to get there. They would have gladly driven any amount of miles it took to nurture hope for a mother and wife with cancer.

Many families have experiences like this. A negative medical diagnosis comes into the family. The situation looks hopeless. And where do you go with such hopelessness? Families frantically cling to hope in these situations. They search out another medical opinion, another doctor. They may drive to world-renowned clinics which are hundreds of miles away from home. They may hear about healing springs in another part of the country. They may hear about places where miracles occur. Hopelessness breeds desperation. A family will go anywhere, pay any price, for the promise of a cure. Desperation takes people down many an interesting path.

Easter 7
Acts 16:16-34

God's Evangelism Plans

The fall of Haile Selassie in 1974 did not bring the kind of peace that the Ethiopians had hoped might follow their somewhat "benevolent" dictator. They had hoped for democracy. They had hoped for freedom. What they got, instead, was a Marxist state that ruled with an iron hand. Repression was everywhere. Persecution was everywhere. The Christian church became a target of this repression and persecution. The almost 20 years of Marxist rule was a very difficult time for the Christians of Ethiopia.

During the waning years of this Marxist rule an Ethiopian pastor named Yadessa addressed an American audience concerning this persecution. He told of churches being closed and of many Christians and Christian leaders being put in prison. He said that there were hardly any churches left open in the western region of Ethiopia where evangelical Christianity had been very strong. But closed church buildings did not close down the church. "Houses became churches," Pastor Yadessa told his audience. Christianity not only survived but thrived and grew under state repression.

Pastor Yadessa reminded his audience that the most significant person to be imprisoned in those years was the president of the church himself, Pastor Gudina. Pastor Gudina was jailed and released several times but he eventually died in prison, Pastor Yadessa reported. He further reported that Pastor Gudina's wife was also imprisoned. "She has adjusted to prison life very well," Pastor Yadessa said. "She sews sweaters for people and distributes Bibles that are sent to her. She and many of the other imprisoned Christians have become great evangelists in the prisons. God has God's own evangelism plans," Pastor Yadessa proclaimed with a smile.

He told another story of God's evangelism planning. At the time of his address to his American audience Pastor Yadessa was the director of evangelism for the Ethiopian Evangelical Church — Mekane Yesus. (Mekane Yesus means "the place of Jesus.") He planned that evangelism leaders from the Addis Ababa area and evangelism leaders from the land to the West that had been so heavily persecuted should meet in a city on the border of the two areas. "Just the logistics of planning the meeting," Pastor Yadessa said, "were extremely difficult. Communication between parties was almost impossible. But," he continued, "when the day for the meeting arrived, somehow, under God's providence, all of us arrived safely."

The meeting, of course, was a bit subversive in light of the state's persecution of the church. The evangelism leaders gathered, therefore, in a simple home in the city. "We were just about to start our meeting," said Pastor Yadessa, "when seven uniformed policemen barged through the door of the house. 'This is an illegal meeting,' the head of the policemen shouted at us. 'You are all under arrest. Come with us at once.' It wasn't long until all of us were safely locked together in prison."

As Pastor Yadessa told the story he indicated that the first hour or two that the leaders were in the jail were moments of great despair. "But then," he said brightening, "we realized that God had given us a great opportunity. Here we were all together in one place with nothing to do but pray together and talk together and think about evangelism together. We found ourselves on a wonderfully unplanned evangelism retreat. God, indeed, has God's own evangelism plans that surprise and surpass our own!"

Day Of Pentecost
Genesis 11:1-9

"Let Us Make A Name For Ourselves"

Narrative Analogy: *Acts 2:1-21*

"When you're No. 1 in the world . . . you're like a god to (people).'' Burt Reynolds made that statement a few years ago. It was reported in the Chicago *Tribune* in an article written by Howard Reich. Mr. Reynolds had come to Chicago with his one-man stage show. The show was titled: "An Evening With Burt Reynolds: The Laughs, the Loves, the Legends, the Lies (Not Necessarily in That Order)." Howard Reich interviewed Mr. Reynolds while Reynolds was in Chicago for the show.

Burt Reynolds, of course, made a marvelous name for himself in show business. From 1977 to 1982 he was the No. 1 box office draw in the world. That's fame all right. That's a name all right. "It was an incredible, extraordinary experience," Reynolds is quoted as saying. "It's almost impossible to explain what it feels like to be that big in the first place. When you're No. 1 in the world (it means) you go to China and Bali, and you get off a plane, and they know you. And they not only know you . . . you're like a god to them."

Burt Reynolds knew what it was like to be No. 1. He knew what it was like to be "like a god" to people. He had achieved a great name for himself. But, as with any *achievement* we make as humans, it can be taken from us in an instant. Being "like a god" to people never lasts. The gods always come crashing down. So did Burt Reynolds. And he was miserable. "You're going to find yourself so unhappy after you're No. 1," he was quoted as saying. "There's only one way to go. You can't stay there, so you're going to drop eventually, and you have to prepare yourself for that."

Mr. Reynolds paid a steep price for falling from his No. 1 ranking. Being god, he discovered, was very hard on his body. "I was tired, depressed, hyperventilating, fainting all the time," he said in the interview. There were rumors at the time that he was dying from AIDS. His friends quickly deserted him! "When you're dropped by everyone the way I was," Reynolds said, "you need an enormous faith in God or Zen or Buddha or whatever. If you don't have something, you're going to go directly to whatever puts you out of this world, whatever pill, whatever you smoke, whatever you can stick in your arm, whatever you can drink."

"There's a saying in the South," said Reynolds, "that no man is a man until his father tells him he is. Well, my father unfortunately didn't tell me until I was 46. So for 46 years I was a little crazy. I was looking for an adult to put his arms around me and say ... 'You're a grown-up; you can start acting differently now.' "

Burt Reynolds had made a great name for himself. Without the love and support of his father and his friends, however, he could sustain neither his status nor his health. "When I fell from my pedestal nobody remembered me," he confessed. "No one called me with offers of work. No one stopped by to see me." He had made a name for himself which attracted all kinds of people into his life. When his name became tarnished, however, the human family on which he so much depended fractured all around him.

Making a name for ourselves can be done in this world. But it comes with a great price. When we make a name for ourself we inevitably get cut off from the very community of people that sustain our life in the first place.

Shy Alice

Alice Hawks was one of the most important members of Christ's Church in Dallas. Pastor Gary Peck had been pastor at Christ's Church for about five years, however, before he even knew Alice's name. That's because Alice was always in the background, always pointing her finger of praise at someone else, never hogging the spotlight for herself. Most people at Christ's Church had seen her around but they had no idea what her name might be or of the broad extent of her service to the congregation.

Alice Hawks had been a member of Christ's Church since the day of her birth. She started to sing in the choir, for example, at an early age and was a regular member of the senior choir. No solos for Alice, of course! When someone would single her out as a member of the choir she always blushed and said, "Oh, anything I do is because of the director. He's just terrific. He could make anybody sing."

When Alice Hawks was in her mid-30s she found her real niche at Christ's Church. The pastor who had served the church at that time asked her if she would become the volunteer coordinator for the congregation. A congregation the size of Christ's Church needed lots of volunteer help in order to make it go. Alice Hawks recognized that this task was just about the perfect fit for her. She had to overcome her shyness about calling people on the telephone but she overcame that soon enough. This was great. She could serve her church and hardly ever leave home. She'd be in the background and that's just where she wanted to be. And she would be doing what she did best. She would match the gifts of the wonderful people of Christ's Church to the needs of the congregation and community.

Alice Hawks was a great volunteer coordinator. Any congregation would have loved to have had her services. Things at Christ's Church ran like clockwork. She always had the right people at the right place at the right time. And all this from the privacy of her own home! Once in a while people would call Alice and thank her for the wonderful job she did in getting volunteers for their area of responsibility. "Don't thank me," Alice would inevitably say. "Thank the people who did the work. They're the ones who deserve the credit."

It took a while for Pastor Peck to realize what a tremendous help Alice Hawks was to his ministry at Christ's Church. Once he really got hold of the scope of her activity he wanted to have a celebration in her honor on the occasion of her completion of 25 years as volunteer coordinator for the congregation. He knew, however, that Alice would have none of it. She wouldn't even show up. She was just too shy.

Pastor Peck, therefore, devised an alternate plan. One Sunday morning, unbeknownst to Alice, he singled her out in the choir after his sermon. He spoke strange words of praise for her. "Alice," he said, "your ministry in this congregation reminds me of the ministry of the Holy Spirit. I read a book in seminary once titled: *The Holy Spirit — Shy Member of the Trinity*. The Holy Spirit is shy because the Spirit never points to self but always points to Jesus. You're kind of like that. You do tons of work for the congregation but you never point to self. You always point to the work of others. We all thank you, Alice, shy as you are, for your spirit-filled ministry in our midst."

Proper 4
Luke 7:1-10

"Only Speak The Word"

Luke is fond of telling stories of faith. In his stories Luke narrates scenes in which trust in the spoken word from God is the very essence of faith. It all begins with an old priest named Zechariah. This is the first story that Luke tells us in his Gospel. One day, Luke writes, the lot fell to Zechariah to enter the temple of the Lord and burn incense. As he was about to perform this sacred task, however, an angel of the Lord appeared to him standing just to the right of the altar. Zechariah was troubled. Fear fell upon him.

The angel spoke words of comfort to Zechariah. "Do not be afraid, Zechariah," the angel said, "for your prayer has been heard. Your wife Elizabeth will bear you a son, and you will name him John" (Luke 1:13). The angel Gabriel went on to announce to Zechariah that his son John would be filled with the Holy Spirit and would make the way ready for the Messiah to come.

Zechariah had heard a word spoken to him from God. Zechariah had heard a word from Gabriel announcing new realities that were to come to pass. Of such stuff is faith composed as Luke tells the story. Faith, or unfaith! Zechariah heard the word from God. He did not believe it! "How will I know that this is so?" Zechariah demanded of the angel (Luke 1:18). "I'm an old man and my wife is old too. How can this word be?"

"I am Gabriel," the angel shot back. "How will I know?" said Zechariah. "I am Gabriel," came the reply. And the angel continued. "... because you did not believe my words, which will be fulfilled in their time, you will become mute, unable to speak, until the day these things occur" (Luke 1:20).

"You did not believe my words." That is the heart of Zechariah's unbelief.

Mary is next in line. Six months into Elizabeth's pregnancy Gabriel spoke words from God to Mary. "Hail, O favored one, the Lord is with you" (Luke 1:28). That was Gabriel's greeting to Mary. Like Zechariah before her, Mary was troubled and afraid at the sound of the angel's voice. Gabriel spoke to her as he had spoken to Zechariah: "Do not be afraid, Mary, for you have found favor with God. And now, you will conceive in your womb and bear a son, and you will name him Jesus" (Luke 1:31).

Mary, like Zechariah, heard a word spoken to her from God. Mary, too, is unsure. "How can this be," she protests, "since I am a virgin?" (Luke 1:35). Gabriel told Mary that it will be because the Holy Spirit will make it happen. Mary was satisfied. She spoke great words of faith. "Here I am," she said, "the servant of the Lord; let it be with me according to your word" (Luke 1:38).

"You did not believe my words," said Gabriel to Zechariah. That is the heart of Zechariah's unfaith. ". . . let it be with me according to your word," were Mary's words to Gabriel. This is the heart of Mary's faith.

Faith is called into being by a word spoken from God. A centurion in Capernaum grasped this reality very well. "Only say the word . . .," the centurion said. Luke presents this rather unlikely fellow, this centurion, this stranger to Israel, this foreigner as a model of faith. "Only say the word . . . ."

"A Great Prophet Has Arisen Among Us"

Narrative Analogy: *1 Kings 17:8-24*

"Shunem: Site of the Prophet Elisha's Resurrection Miracle." If they had had road signs in the days of old this might have been the sign that welcomed you to Shunem. All the people of Shunem and all the people in the cities around Shunem surely knew of Elisha's miraculous feat. This was an area known for its prophets!

Elisha's prophetic forerunner, Elijah, was the first prophet to raise a young man to life. It happened in Zarephath (1 Kings 17:8-24). Perhaps it is not surprising that Elisha also raised a young man to life. We are told, after all, that Elisha inherited a *double share* of Elijah's spirit!

In a story told in 2 Kings 4 we hear that Elijah came to Shunem one day and had a bite to eat at the home of a wealthy woman. Since there were no fast food restaurants in Elisha's day, he stopped quite often at the house of the Shunammite woman to get something to eat. The woman sensed that Elisha was a holy one of God. So she persuaded her husband to fix up a permanent guest room for Elisha. She invited Elisha to stop and stay with them whenever he passed through Shunem. And he did. Free room and board is a pretty good deal, after all!

Now Elisha was an honorable man. He thought he should really give this woman some kind of gift. He told his servant Gehazi to ask the Shunammite woman what gift he might give to her. Gehazi went. He discovered that the woman was quite content with what she had. She asked for nothing. "But there must be something we can give this woman," Elisha insisted to Gehazi. Then Gehazi had a wonderful idea. "This woman has no child and her husband is old," he said to Elisha.

77

Elisha got the point. He announced to the woman of Shunem that, "At this season, when the time comes round, you shall embrace a son" (2 Kings 4:16). And it came to pass just as Elisha had promised. One day years later, the son of the woman of Shunem went out among the reapers to be with his father. Suddenly he began to complain bitterly. "Oh, my head, my head!" he shrieked.

"Carry the lad to his mother," the father ordered. The reapers did so. The boy lay on his mother's lap until noon, and then he died. The Shunammite woman carried her son straightway to Elisha's guest room and laid him on Elisha's very own bed. She then set out to Mt. Carmel determined to find Elisha. When she found the prophet she fell before him and took hold of his feet. "Did I ask my Lord for a son?" she pleaded. "Did I not say, 'Do not mislead me'?" (2 Kings 4:28).

Elisha got the point. He returned to Shunem, went to his room where the dead boy lay, shut the door and began to pray. Elisha then stretched himself upon the boy and breathed his breath into him. Soon the child sneezed seven times and then opened his eyes. "Take your son," Elisha said to the woman of Shunem.

"Shunem: Site of the Prophet Elisha's Resurrection Miracle." Thus a sign at the city gate might have read. The city of Nain was just a stone's throw down the road from Shunem. The citizens of Nain undoubtedly basked in Shunem's glory. They, too, believed themselves to live in a land where prophets do miracles.

Forgiven Much!

The life of a prostitute is a hateful way of life. Debra, a woman whose father had thrown her out on the street, quickly came to hate herself for what she had become. She often thought of taking her own life. In modern psychological parlance we would say that Debra had lost all of her self-esteem. She was a woman desperate for affection, desperate for someone, anyone, to treat her with dignity. She just could not see herself as a person of worth. No surprise there. No one had ever treated her as a person of worth.

Then one day when Debra was walking through her village she spotted a crowd of people coming her way. Her immediate thought was to get her worthless self out of the crowd's way. Something held her in place, however. She could soon see that the crowd was gathered around a storyteller. As the storyteller came closer his eyes met her eyes. She looked down immediately. It was instinct. Habit. Who was she to look anyone straight in the eye? The storyteller reached out his hand and cupped her chin gently in his strong hand. He lifted her head and looked her directly in the eye. He invited her to join the crowd.

And then the storyteller proceeded to tell a story. We know it as the story of the prodigal son. Debra quickly identified with this prodigal son. He, too, had fallen from grace. He wound up in a pigpen far from home. She recognized the man in the pigpen. She understood just how he felt. That's the kind of life she lived. She could just as well live in a pigpen. Then the outer circumstances of her body would mirror the inner feelings of her soul.

What would become of the pigpen man she wondered? Soon she had her answer. The pigpen man decided to go back home to his father with words of repentance and tears of remorse. To her astonishment the father ran out to meet the pigpen man. "Quickly, bring a robe," the father said, "the best one — and put it on him; put a ring on his finger and sandals on his feet. And get the fatted calf and kill it, and let us eat and celebrate; for this son of mine was dead and is alive again; he was lost and is found!" (Luke 15:22-24).

This story captivated Debra. At first she wondered what her father would do if she tried to return home. She knew the answer to that question all too well! She knew something about human fathers after all. The father in this story, however, was clearly a different kind of father than any she had ever known or experienced.

Debra was taken up into this story. She remembered how the storyteller had lifted her chin, looked into her eyes and asked her to join the crowd. He acted toward her just the way the father in the story acted toward his son. Then it dawned upon her. The storyteller was telling this story as a story about God. God is like a father who embraces a man from the pigpen. So it could be with her! "God is like a father who embraces me, pigpen and all," she thought to herself.

Weeks later this storyteller returned to her town. Simon, a Pharisee, invited him to dinner. This would be Debra's chance to say thanks to the man whose story brought acceptance and worth into her life. She would crash Simon's party. She would wash the storyteller's feet.

Proper 7
Galatians 3:23-29

The Collapsing Circle

Allan Nelson is a consultant to business operations throughout the world. Allan Nelson is also a deeply committed Christian. He ofttimes walks a fine line through life as he seeks to live out his Christian faith in the midst of a variety of culture clashes. One such clash for Mr. Nelson took place in 1978 in a visit to Soweto in South Africa. In a profound and exciting way he experienced in this land afar off the collapsing of a circle of innate suspicion and hostility.

Mr. Nelson was in South Africa on a business trip to advise American companies as to how they might best respond to pressures to do something positive in this world of apartheid. As a church-going man he determined to go to church somewhere in the city on Sunday morning. Quite intentionally he sought a place to worship in a black South African congregation. He wasn't at all sure he would be welcome in such a congregation. But he knew his scriptures. He knew that in Jesus Christ the barriers that separated people should be broken down. He hoped he would be accepted.

Allan was told that there was such a congregation just five blocks from his hotel. As he and a friend whom he invited to go with him walked those five blocks to church he was reminded at each step of the racial barriers that separated the races in South Africa in those days. "Whites Only" and "Blacks Only" signs were everywhere. There was no mingling of the races anywhere. It became more clear to him than ever that white and black in South Africa were divided by huge walls of practiced hatred. Maybe he shouldn't go to a black church after all. Allan began to second guess his decision. But then the church loomed just ahead. He consciously submerged his fears of apartheid and nourished his hopes for a new kind of world where all the baptized are one in Christ Jesus.

Allan and his friend arrived early. They simply entered the empty church, found a seat, and waited. Slowly the members of the all black congregation began to file in. No one sat very close to them. Not close at all! In fact when the sanctuary was filled there was a large circle of empty seats that surrounded the two white Americans. Here they were. Two white faces surrounded by a sea of black faces as isolated as an island in the ocean. A lump came to Allan's throat. His fears now drowned out his hopes. Perhaps it was too much to expect that the circle of hatred could collapse even in a Christian church.

And then, before the service started, a woman got up and began to sing "Amazing Grace." Allan described her voice as one of the most beautiful he had ever heard. Allan was moved by her singing. It was beautiful. So beautiful, in fact, that when she started to sing verse two some great impulse from within prompted him to join his tenor voice to her song. They were singing. Just the two of them black and white in harmony.

An old woman from the back of the church came forward and touched him. "Jesus," she said softly. That was the one bond between them. And then Mr. Nelson committed an illegal act. He embraced the woman. They both wept. Suddenly, the circle of emptiness around them collapsed. People shoved up against Allan from every side. His hopes had won out over his fears. There was, indeed, one church, one baptism! Allan Nelson now says that this event changed his life forever.

Proper 8
Luke 9:51-62

He Set His Face

Narrative Analogy: *cf. the role of Jerusalem in Luke-Acts*

He had just finished feeding the 5,000 men plus women and children when he asked them the question (Luke 9:10-17). In this context of feeding people (cf. Luke 24:28-35) Jesus asked his disciples, "Who do the crowds say that I am?" (Luke 9:18). We stand here at a turning point in Luke's story of Jesus. In earlier stories of Jesus' baptism, genealogy, temptation and a sabbath in his hometown synagogue Luke has given us all kinds of clues as to the identity of Jesus. After that there comes action. Jesus healed people. He forgave sinners. He called disciples. He challenged sabbath laws and so on. It's time now to return to the question of identity. Do even the disciples understand who this man is? Does anyone really understand?

The disciples answered Jesus question by stating the opinions of some in the crowds. Jesus' then zeroes in on the disciples themselves. "But who do you say that I am?" (Luke 9:20). "The Messiah of God," Peter answered.

And then Jesus did a surprising thing. He acknowledged that Peter had the right answer to his question. But he told the disciples not to tell anyone the truth of his identity. The coming of the Messiah would move Israel from one degree of glory to another. But Jesus was not to be this Messiah of glory. Jesus was to be a Messiah on a cross. Jesus tells it straight in a new revelation of his identity. "The Son of Man must undergo great suffering, and be rejected by the elders, chief priests, and scribes, and be killed and on the third day be raised" (Luke 9:22).

The disciples must have been stunned. They had glory on their minds, too. But, no, the way of this Messiah was to be a way of suffering for him and for the disciples. "If any want to become my followers, let them deny themselves and take up their cross daily and follow me" (Luke 9:23). The disciples never could get this through their heads. In the story of the transfiguration which Luke tells next we hear Jesus discussing the departure he would accomplish in Jerusalem. Jesus, that is, was discussing with Moses and Elijah his way to Jerusalem, his way to the cross. And the disciples? They wanted to build booths and live on this mountain of glory and transfiguration forever. They did not know what they were saying, Luke tells us.

This hardness of heart of the disciples appears again when they all come down from the Mount of Transfiguration. A man comes to Jesus in order that Jesus might heal his son who is possessed by a demon. "I begged your disciples to cast it out, but they could not," the father says to Jesus. Jesus proceeds to wonder aloud about the faithless disciples. He tells them again, therefore, of his mission. "Let these words sink into your ears," he tells them, "The Son of Man is going to be betrayed into human hands." Sadly Luke tells us of the disciples that, ". . . they did not understand this saying; its meaning was concealed from them, so they could not perceive it" (Luke 9:44-45). The disciples prove the truth of this statement by turning to a discussion among themselves about which one of them was the greatest. They're still thinking of glory!

Jesus has revealed that he must go to Jerusalem to suffer, to die and to be raised again. The disciples don't get it at all. With his heart heavy with the suffering that lay ahead, therefore, and with his mind puzzled by disciples who failed to understand, Jesus set his face to go to Jerusalem.

Proper 9
2 Kings 5:1-14 (15-19)

"God's Gonna Trouble The Water"

"What difference is a little water going to make anyway?" Ken Taufler thundered at his friend Jim Kaufmann for the hundredth time.

A little background information: Jim Kaufmann and Ken Taufler worked together in an insurance agency. The men had built a good working relationship with each other forged through many long hours spent on joint projects. Through it all, Jim and Ken became good friends. Eventually, their families got into the act as well. Their families had a lot in common.

There were also some important aspects of their lives, however, that they did not hold in common. The most important difference between them was in the area of religion. Jim Kaufmann and his wife Denice were deeply committed Christian folks. Ken Taufler had never even darkened the door of a church. He had no Christian training as a youth and he didn't want any as an adult! Gena, Ken's wife, followed her husband's lead in this area. So, neither one of them attended church.

Jim Kaufmann was troubled by his friend's indifference to the faith. They spoke about it often. "Can't you just try church for a while?" Jim challenged Ken. "What can it hurt? Come to our congregation. We'd love to have you. I think you'll find that it is a meaningful experience."

After much badgering, and to Jim's great surprise, his inviting attitude finally worked. Ken Taufler and his wife Gena promised to give church a whirl. They would come regularly for two months and see what would come of it all. Ken felt very awkward about it all at first. He really didn't know much more about Christianity than what you hear and read in the media. Ken found the actual living, breathing community of Christian people to be quite different from what he had imagined. The people were very friendly and supportive. But also, to his great surprise, Ken found the Bible stories and the sermons to be very meaningful to him. He was touched by the words and works of Jesus. He began to realize that his life had a spiritual void which Jesus addressed quite directly.

At work one day Ken Taufler asked his friend Jim what it would take for him and Gena to join the church. Jim Kaufmann could hardly believe his ears. "That's wonderful," he blurted out to Ken. "You really want to join. Great! It's pretty simple really. You need to contact the pastor first to find out when the next membership class is to begin. After you're instructed you'll be baptized and you'll be a member of our church."

"Baptized?" Ken queried. "You mean I would have to be baptized, soaked with some meaningless water, in order to join the church? I don't think I could do that. This baptism stuff looks an awful lot like magic to me. What difference is a little water going to make anyway?"

"The water is a visible and concrete way for God's love to touch you and it provides a concrete place for you to say your 'Yes' to God," Jim replied. "Jesus commanded us to be baptized you know. I kind of look at the water part as a tangible sign of God's presence and God's promise."

Ken Taufler wasn't convinced. It was the part about the water that was the real stumbling block for him. "Whoever heard of such a thing?" he mused to Jim. "Get washed with water, say yes, and then you're a Christian? What good is this water? What difference is a little water going to make anyway?"

Proper 10
Luke 10:25-37

A Model For The Good Life

Narrative Analogy: *Luke 16:15; 18:9*

We all remember Desert Storm. The United States and her allies came out on the winning side of a tense battle with the Iraq of Saddam Hussein. When Desert Storm came to an end after tense months of waiting and a few short days of actual fighting it was time to take stock of things. The most grievous task was counting up the dead and notifying loved ones back home. Each unit had to account for all of its personnel. Who was alive? Who had been killed? Who was missing in action? Private Benny Blades was one of those listed as missing in action in his unit. There was no body to prove evidence of death. No one could remember seeing him wounded. His disappearance was a mystery.

Mystery turned into miracle one day about a week after the fighting had ceased when Private Benny Blades was picked up along the road by some soldiers returning from the front. The men and women in his unit were overjoyed with Benny's return. That night they held a great welcoming ceremony for Benny. His comrades wanted to hear his story. What happened to him? How did he survive? What had happened to his legs? Benny told his story. He had been wounded by Iraqi fire. Took several bullets in his legs. Unable to move he could only lie on the field of battle and hope that someone would rescue him. On the second day of his ordeal he was rescued — by an Iraqi soldier. Groans and laughter followed Benny's words. How could this be, the soldiers wondered?

"I talked to the soldier myself," Benny went on. "His name was Ahmad. He said he saw me lying on the field of battle from his battlefield outpost. What's more he saw two of our jeeps pass fairly close to where I was without stopping to help."

87

What Ahmad had seen were a chaplain and a medic. The chaplain slowed his jeep as he came by the area and saw a soldier lying there. He was a bit afraid of the area, however. Furthermore, he was to hold services back at the base very shortly. He just didn't have the time to stop. The other jeep that Ahmad had seen was driven by a medic. The medic had been called north for a serious emergency. It was on his way that he spotted the soldier lying in the field. But this was just *one* wounded man. He was on his way to tend *many*. And so the medic, too, left Benny lay.

Benny continued his story. "Ahmad said that when he saw our jeeps pass me by he thought he'd better do something himself. He came to me in his vehicle, tended my wounds, then drove me behind their lines to a medical unit. He ordered the medical personnel there to look after my legs. They did a good job. Ahmad came around a number of times to make sure that I was getting proper treatment. Isn't that something? Who would ever have believed that there was a good Iraqi soldier out there who would save my life? He's a real hero to me I tell you. Without his help I'd be dead. Ahmad will always live in my heart as a kind of model of the good life."

There was stunned silence among Benny's comrades as he finished his story. Finally Terry Slawson spoke up. He spoke for just about everyone in the room. "Sorry Benny," Terry began, "but I don't believe a word of it. I really don't. There is just no such thing as a good Iraqi soldier." Everyone cheered!

Proper 11
Luke 10:38-42

Choices

Narrative Analogy: *Luke 1:26-38; 11:27-28; 24:1-11*

She was elected to high office some time ago. Let's call
her Beverly Washington. She was the first woman Lieutenant
Governor ever elected in her state. Such a first brought much
deserved media attention. There were many demands for photo
opportunities and interviews. Beverly Washington had never
experienced the limelight quite like this before.

One of the interviews with Lt. Governor Washington was
conducted by a much younger woman who was obviously taken
with the Lt. Governor's success. "I see you have a degree in
law from Harvard," the interviewer began. "You must have
had a family which really supported your dreams for higher
education. Not many women were encouraged to go to college and law school in the 20s and 30s. You seem to be the
exception to the rule."

"I'm no exception at all," Beverly Washington replied.
"My father's attitude was that boys should go on to school
and girls should get married and raise a family. I was lucky
that he let me finish high school. After high school I simply
determined to go to college. There would be no financial help.
There would be no moral or family support. But I decided.
I thought it was unfair to hold women back the way my father
wanted to hold my sisters and me back. So I decided, packed
my bags, and left for college."

"Very good," said the impressed interviewer, "I guess you
were blazing trails for women a long time ago. How then did
you get started in politics? Not many women ran for public
office in the days you first ran."

"That's true," Lt. Governor Washington responded. "It
certainly wasn't easy. It wasn't easy finding a job as a lawyer

either. There weren't many women lawyers in those days and no one would hire me. I took all kinds of odd jobs to support myself and our family in those early years. That's when I decided that there was something wrong with a system that could discriminate against women in such a way. So I began to wonder how I might change the system. I concluded that the best way to change the system was to get into elective politics. I would become part of the system! Then I could change it. But, of course, that was more easily said than done. It was hard, for example, just trying to get enough signatures on my petition to run for office. The office was county auditor. It took me six months to get the necessary signatures. But I did it. I got beat in the election, of course. Bad! I lost my first three tries but I finally did get elected county treasurer. I knew I was bucking the system. I knew I was blazing a new trail for women. But I had decided in the face of much opposition that this is what I had to do. I decided and I stuck with my decision."

"And here you are the newly-elected Lt. Governor," the interviewer interjected. "It must be a wonderful feeling. You continue to prove the critics wrong. Do you have any advice for women who might be inspired by your example to run for public office?"

"Go for it," Ms. Washington shot back. "You've got to decide for yourself. All the old rules may be lined up against you. Even friends and family may not always support you. So, you've got to want it very badly and be willing to pay the price. The most important thing is that you must decide for yourself. Then stick with your decision. Choose your path and don't look back."

Proper 12
Colossians 2:6-15 (16-19)

Disarming Evil

People Of The Lie: The Hope For Healing Human Evil
is one of Dr. M. Scott Peck's most intriguing books. In his
work with patients as a psychiatrist and a Christian, Dr. Peck
has come to see that there are people who are simply evil. He
thinks that this evil needs to be studied by scientists as well
as known by theologians. Until we can name and identify evil
at work among us we have no way of disarming its power.

Early in his book Dr. Peck tells one of the stories from
his counseling practice that helped lead him to see that evil
is a genuine reality in the world. He calls it, "The Case Of
Bobby And His Parents." Bobby was a 15-year-old boy who
was sent by the court to see Dr. Peck because his grades in
school were falling precipitously, he was depressed and he had
an accident with a stolen car. Dr. Peck met with Bobby and
heard his story. He noticed that Bobby's face was dull and
expressionless, the kind of face one sees in people in a con-
centration camp. Dr. Peck was alarmed by what he saw. He
was even more alarmed by what he heard. He learned that Bobby's older brother, Stuart, had committed suicide in June of
last year. Stuart had shot himself in the head with a .22 caliber
rifle. Stuart's suicide had clearly been the cause for Bobby's
academic slide and personal depression. But there was more.
At Christmas time Bobby's parents gave him a .22 rifle. "Isn't
that the same kind of gun your brother used to kill himself?"
an amazed Dr. Peck said to Bobby. "It wasn't the same *kind*
of gun," Bobby replied. "It was the same gun."

Dr. Peck was stunned. Bobby's parents were all but telling him that the whole matter with Stuart was his fault and
things would be best if he would commit suicide too. Dr. Peck

91

called the parents to his office. They seemed to be quite normal, blue collar, church-going, hard-working folks. Dr. Peck confronted them with their deed. "Don't you see that giving Bobby this gun was like telling him to go out and kill himself?" Dr. Peck inquired. The parents, Dr. Peck tells us, could see no such thing. They were blind to the consequences of their own deeds.

In his continued work with Bobby and his parents Dr. Peck began to formulate the thesis that these parents were evil people. He then cites a law of child development: "When a child is grossly confronted by significant evil in its parents, it will most likely misinterpret the situation and believe that the evil resides in the self." Bobby, that is, was in the clutches of evil powers. This evil resided in his parents whom Dr. Peck discovered to be, as his book title states, "People of the lie" (cf. John 8:44-45). They were people who could simply not tell the truth about themselves. That is Dr. Peck's definition of evil. Evil people deceive others by building layer upon layer of self-deception around themselves. Evil people are not the same as sinful people. It is not their sins in themselves that distinguish between evil people and sinful people. The difference is that evil people refuse to acknowledge any fault at all in their character.

Not being able to see and acknowledge their own faults was the characteristic of Bobby's parents. As such, Dr. Peck suggests, they were evil people. And evil, he tells us, can only be overcome with raw power. Evil, in other words, is a force that has to be conquered. Anywhere that evil rules in this world, therefore, such evil has to be disarmed.

Proper 13
Luke 12:13-21

Great Reversals

Narrative Analogy: *Luke 1:46-55 (53); 4:18-19; 6:20-26 et al.*

The theme of poverty, riches, possessions and the realm of God is a constant theme of Luke. It begins with Mary's song. Mary had an encounter with an angel. "You will bear a son and call his name Jesus," the angel announced. "Let it be with me according to your word," said Mary. Elizabeth, Mary's relative, blessed Mary for her trust that God's word of promise would be fulfilled. And then Mary sang a song. Mary's song may just well be the central song of Luke's entire gospel. Luke tells many stories in his gospel that are best understood as comments on her song!

Mary's song sings of a God of great reversals. This God has high regard for a lowly maiden. This God scatters the proud and puts down the mighty from their thrones. The high are made low and the low are exalted. This God, furthermore, fills the hungry with good things and sends the rich away empty-handed. That's the kind of God that Mary sings about it. A God of great reversals. A God who makes the rich poor and the poor rich.

Jesus sings a similar song in his hometown synagogue in Nazareth. During the worship service that day Jesus was given the scroll of Isaiah that he might read it to the congregation. "The Spirit of the Lord is upon me," Jesus read, "because he has anointed me to bring good news to the poor. He has sent me to proclaim release to the captives and recovery of sight to the blind, to let the oppressed go free, to proclaim the year of the Lord's favor" (Luke 4:18-19). Isaiah had prophesied that God would send a spirit-filled servant who would bring a great reversal to human affairs.

After he had finished reading from the Isaiah scroll, Jesus gave it to the attendant and sat down. Every eye in the synagogue was fixed upon him. Jesus spoke. "Today this scripture has been fulfilled in your hearing," he said. *He* was the spirit-filled servant of whom Isaiah had prophesied. *He* was the one who would bring great reversals to life in fulfillment of Mary's song. *He* was the one who brought good news to the poor.

"Blessed are you poor." We should not be surprised at these words of Jesus to his disciples. In Luke 6:20-26 Jesus also speaks of great reversals. The poor will be blessed. The hungry will be satisfied. The weeping ones shall laugh. Those who are persecuted for righteousness' sake will rejoice. Reversals work the other way as well. The weak of the earth will be blessed but the mighty of the earth shall be filled with woe. Woe to the rich. Woe to those who are full now. Woe to those who laugh now. Woe to those of whom the world now speaks well.

John the Baptist watched Jesus' ministry from afar. John wondered about Jesus. Was he really the promised Messiah? John sent some of his disciples to Jesus with just this question. "Are you the one who is to come, or are we to wait for another?" John's disciples asked Jesus on John's behalf (Luke 7:21). Jesus had an answer for John. "Go and tell John what you have seen and heard," he instructs John's disciples, "the blind receive their sight, the lame walk, the lepers are cleansed, the deaf hear, the dead are raised, and the poor have good news brought to them" (Luke 7:22). The "great reversals" have begun. That's Jesus' word to John.

Today's story from Luke is a story in this lineage. A great reversal takes place. The rich man is sent away empty. The poor hear good news!

Proper 14
Hebrews 11:1-3, 8-16

The Laughter Of Faith

God called Sarah, too! We talk so much about God's call to Abraham that we can easily forget that God called Sarah as well. The story is told in Genesis 17. This old story begins with God's call to Abraham. It then moves to Sarah. "As for Sarah," God says, "she shall no longer be called Sarai but Sarah shall be her name." "I will bless her ..." God promises, "and she shall give rise to nations; kings of people shall come from her" (Genesis 17:16).

We can only imagine the solemnity of the moment when God made this promise to Abraham and Sarah. Abraham broke the solemnity. He fell on his face laughing at the very thought of God's promise. "Can a child be born to a man who is 100 years old?" Abraham laughed to himself. "Can Sarah, who is 90 years old, bear a child?" Abraham's laughter, it turns out, is the laughter of unbelief. He doesn't believe that God can keep this promise. The Lord has to scold Abraham a bit for his unseemly laughter. "No," God says firmly, "your wife shall bear you a son, and you shall name him Isaac" (Genesis 17:19). The Lord, it seems, also has a sense of humor. The name Isaac means: "he laughs."

Very soon thereafter the Lord visited Abraham in the guise of three messengers. Abraham and Sarah scurried around like mad making their home suitable for a visit from the Lord. They put on their finest spread. As the meal begins we hear that the Lord has made this appearance in order to speak with Sarah. "Where is Sarah your wife?" the Lord said to Abraham. Abraham had laughed off God's promise to Sarah. But the Lord perseveres. The Lord speaks the promise again in Sarah's hearing. "I will surely return to you in due season and your wife Sarah shall have a son" (Genesis 18:10).

This time it was Sarah who laughed. "After I have grown old, and my husband is old, shall I have pleasure?" she mused (Genesis 18:12). Sarah joined her husband in the laughter of unbelief. For the Lord, however, this was not a laughing matter. The Lord was angry with all this laughter of unbelief. "Is anything too wonderful for the Lord?" the Lord says in reprimand of Sarah's laughter. Sarah protested. "I did not laugh," she said to the Lord in fear. "Oh yes you did laugh," the Lord replied (Genesis 18:14-15).

Now a little laughter cannot dissuade the Lord. The Lord had made a promise to Sarah. The Lord kept that promise. The Lord means what the Lord says! Sarah did conceive and bear a son. What joy this son must have brought into the life of Abraham and Sarah! They named him "laughter," Isaac, as the one who promised had instructed them.

But we're not done with the laughing. Now it was Sarah's turn to laugh. "God has brought laughter for me; everyone who hears will laugh with me," Sarah said. "Who would ever have said to Abraham that Sarah would nurse children? Yet I have born him a son in his old age" (Genesis 21:6-7). Sarah's laughter here is clearly a sign of her faith. At least that's how the author of the book of Hebrews understands the story. Sarah's laughter has turned from the laughter of unbelief to the laughter of belief. She has heard the promise. She has conceived. She has given birth. She has believed it all. And she has laughed about it all. As Sarah is our witness, what better response can be given to this promise-making, promise-keeping Lord?

The Faithful Harlot

What's a bad girl like you doing in a list like this? The author of the book of Hebrews tells of a great cloud of witnesses that surround us in our own faith walk. The usual biblical heroes and heroines are there. The biggest surprise in the list is Rahab. Rahab was not an Israelite after all. She was a harlot who plied her trade in pre-Israelite Jericho. Who is this woman anyway? And what is she doing in a list like this?

Rahab's story is told in the Old Testament book of Joshua. In the story we hear that Jericho was next on Joshua's list of cities to be conquered. Joshua sent two spies into Jericho to size up the task of triumphing over this great city. After sneaking into the city they were made welcome in the house of a harlot. That's how Rahab entered Israel's story.

The king of Jericho had spies of his own, of course. They informed him that Rahab was housing two spies of the people of Israel. The king of Jericho, therefore, sent a message to Rahab calling upon her to take a great patriotic action and give up the spies. But the king's message had come to late. Rahab had already hidden the spies on her roof. She told the king's messengers that two unknown men had come to her house but that they had left the city before the gate was closed the night before. "You can probably catch them if you hurry," she told them.

Then Rahab went to the Israelite spies on her roof. The intent of her mission is astounding. She confesses to them her faith in the God who has brought them here! "I know that the Lord has given you the land," she said to them, "and that dread of you has fallen on us, and that all the inhabitants of the land melt in fear before you. For we have heard how the

Lord dried up the water of the Red Sea before you when you came out of Egypt . . . . The Lord your God is indeed God in heaven above and on earth below" (Joshua 2:9-11). The author of Hebrews has it right. Rahab is a woman of faith. She has heard the stories of the Lord's deliverance and she has believed. In Rahab we meet a harlot who believes; a sinner who is a saint.

Now Rahab had a request for the spies sent by Joshua. "Give me a sign of good faith," she says to them, "that you will spare my father and mother, my brother and sisters and all who belong to them and deliver our lives from death" (Joshua 2:12-13). The spies agreed. "Our life for yours!" they promise her.

Rahab then let the men down a rope from her window that they might escape the city. She gave them complete escape instructions. The spies promised again that they would remember their oath to protect Rahab and her family. They gave Rahab a scarlet cord and told her to let it hang from the window of their escape. This would be a sign of protection for Rahab and her family would all be spared because of the sign. "According to your words, so be it," Rahab declared (Joshua 2:21). How nearly do Mary's words in response to the angel's promise match those of Rahab! Mary said, ". . . let it be with me according to your word" (Luke 1:38). Was Rahab Mary's teacher in faith?

Joshua and the army of Israel soon conquered the city of Jericho. The sign of faith, the scarlet cord, hung from Rahab's window. Rahab and her family were saved by her faith. Faith bloomed in a powerful way in this person we would least expect. That's what Rahab is doing in a list like this.

Proper 16
Luke 13:10-17

A Bent Over Woman

The woman with the battered face. Several years back that battered face was splashed all over the media. The woman's name was Hedda Nussbaum. She came to public attention as a dramatic witness for the prosecution in the death of her adopted daughter, Lisa.

Hedda Nussbaum was a vulnerable person already in her early years. She says that when she was a child, "I just went where I was taken." She just obeyed orders. Not surprisingly, she fell in love with a man who loved to give orders. His name was Joel Steinberg. He was an attorney. "I just loved to hear him talk," Hedda said of Joel. "Basically, I worshipped him. He was the most wonderful man I had ever met. I believed he had supernatural, godlike power." Friends of Hedda Nussbaum described her as a person in search of a god. She thought she had found a god in Joel Steinberg.

Hedda moved in with Joel! Two years later the beatings began. Joel Steinberg was an abusive person. The system that was created in the pairing of Hedda Nussbaum and Joel Steinberg was a very sick system. Hedda needed a god. Joel was a controlling and manipulative man. They chose each other. It was to be a fatal choice!

Joel Steinberg had Hedda Nussbaum totally under his control. He told her where she could go, whom she could talk to, what she should do at work and so on. He forbade her to see her parents. And, he beat her. She reported finally that he hit her violently time and time again. Her spleen was ruptured by one of his blows and she had to have it removed. Her knee was damaged, she was burned, her sexual organs were beaten with a broomstick, some of her teeth were knocked out, her hair was pulled out. A New York City doctor described Hedda's case as, "absolutely the worst case of wife battering I've ever seen. She was a slave," he said, "totally submissive to this man, with no ability or will to save her own daughter."

Hedda Nussbaum was a nobody. She was a thoroughly "bent over" woman. "I'm a piece of ----," Joel made her write over and over. She wrote it and she believed it.

The tragedy that brought Hedda Nussbaum and Joel Steinberg to the courtroom and to public knowledge was the death of their daughter, Lisa. Mr. Steinberg was going out one evening. Lisa wondered if he was going to take her with him. Hedda told her to go to the bathroom and ask him. She did. Joel Steinberg proceeded to knock her unconscious. Hedda didn't know what to do with this lifeless body. "Don't worry," Joel said, "just let her sleep. I will get her up when I get back."

Hedda waited. She was confused. She was so dependent on Joel's every command, so convinced of his healing power, that she did nothing for Lisa. She was simply paralyzed. Consequently, Lisa died three days later. Hedda could have saved her. But to act on her own would have been an act of disloyalty to Steinberg. She was not a free person. She was not free to act. She was, indeed, a "bent over" woman with not an ounce of self-esteem left in her.

And Hedda is not alone in this world. In the United States alone 1.8 million women are battered every year. Some form of violence occurs in 25 percent of all marriages. On and on the statistics roll. There are "bent over" women everywhere. Who shall stand them *straight* again?

Proper 17
Luke 14:1, 7-14

The Uninvited

Narrative Analogy: *Luke 14:12-14, 15-24*

"I was the guy that never got chosen by either side." The speaker of these words was a man by the name of Mack Thorson. He was reflecting on the ordinary and basically unimportant events of his life. "You know what I mean," he said in earnest to the group gathered in Pastor Willingham's office. "There's always one or two guys that don't get chosen when you're kids getting ready to play ball. You understand me pretty well if you know that I was one of those who never got chosen. I never got invited to anything. I was always left out. I was, after all, one of the smallest kids in school. I didn't look like much of an athlete and, to tell you the truth, I really wasn't very good at sports. Still, it hurt to be left out all the time."

"But playing ball wasn't the worst of it. It really started at home. I was the youngest of four children and I just didn't get very much attention. Mom and Dad were kind of tired of raising kids by the time I came along. They didn't have much time for me. I just kind of grew up thinking that I wasn't a very important person. I still think that. I mean, look at me. I've got a small job at a big factory. Anybody could do what I do! I guess I'm the original 'little guy.' To tell you the truth, I can't imagine that anyone could feel less important than I feel. Who cares about me anyway?"

The ten or so people in Pastor Willingham's office listened intently to Mack Thorson's story. But, nobody said a word. This was the first night that this group had met with their pastor. It was billed as a four-week session for people with low self-esteem. Pastor Willingham had begun the first session by simply inviting everyone to tell a bit of their life story. Mack

101

had been the first to speak. Pastor Willingham said a few words in response to Mack's story and then invited Sophia Melendez to speak.

There was a hush in the room while Ms. Melendez summoned up the courage to speak. "Ugly duckling," Sophia finally blurted out with her face half buried in her handkerchief. "That's what I was. That's what I am. I've always been the ugly duckling. I started wearing glasses in the third grade. I had big braces on my teeth for a couple of years. I could hardly stand to look at myself in the mirror. I was just so darned ugly. It's hard for me to talk about it even today."

"Needless to say, I didn't have many friends. I was ashamed to try to make friends with anybody. On the other hand, when kids approached me, I didn't really trust them. 'Why are you coming around me?' I always thought to myself. 'Nobody else cares about me. Why should you?' "

"Since this is a church group I should probably say that I've never felt very important in God's eyes either. I sort of grew up in the church, but I left it for a long time. I just didn't feel welcome. I didn't feel like I belonged. I'm just now trying to make my way back. What's the point, you know? We always used to sing, 'Jesus Loves Me.' I sang it, but I never believed it. Nobody else loved me, why should Jesus? I'm sure that my life is of no importance to God whatsoever. I don't like to say it that way this being a church group and all, but that's the way it has always seemed to me. I'm sort of surprised, you know, that Pastor Willingham invited me to be here."

Bearing The Cross

At long last, Laura McDermott had fulfilled her lifelong dream. All she could ever think of doing with her life since she was a kid was to be a doctor. Now no one in the McDermott family had ever been to college before, let alone medical school. Her parents, therefore, were constantly reminding her of the obstacles in her path. "Are you sure you know what you are getting into?" her parents would quiz her periodically. Laura's friends pointed to other obstacles. "Are you sure you want to put yourself through that much schooling? It's really hard work. Is it worth it?"

Laura McDermott persisted. She got through college and medical school. Laura McDermott was a doctor at last. She had lived her dream. But the dream soon turned into a nightmare. Dr. McDermott was hired to work with a group of physicians. That's exactly as she had imagined it. She would be one of two general practitioners in a group which included many specialists as well. An ideal work environment she thought. And it started out well. Soon enough, however, problems began to emerge.

The first problem that faced Dr. McDermott was that she was one of only two women doctors on the clinic staff. The other G.P. was a man with a few years' experience. It became clear to her quite soon that he was getting far more referrals than she was from the other physicians at the clinic. What was even worse, however, was that when she referred patients to some of the specialists they would quite often check out her referral with the other G.P. Her peers clearly did not trust her judgment.

Laura did not know what to make of this situation. Was it because she was young that this happened or because she was a woman? She tried to find out. She asked hard questions around the clinic. But she got no straight answers. It was like a conspiracy of silence had formed around her. Dr. McDermott was devastated.

The other problem was that she just didn't like some of the doctors with whom she worked. They were just not nice people she thought. Friction was in the air at the clinic all the time because of the personalities that worked there. It was not a good work atmosphere. She hated to go to work each day. The whole situation was just awful.

The situation got so bad, in fact, that Dr. McDermott just had to talk to somebody about it. At her church she had met and made friends with another woman about her age, Doris Pagel, who worked for the local chamber of commerce. Laura thought that Doris might have some insights for her about the kind of people that made up their town. Maybe she had the situation figured out all wrong. She hoped Doris could help.

Dr. McDermott took Doris Pagel out for dinner one night and told her sad tale. Doris' first reaction caught Laura by surprise. "Nobody ever said being a doctor would be easy," she said. Laura assured Doris that she knew that. It's just that so many other things had entered the picture that surprised her with the reality of just how hard it was for her to serve God by living out her vocation as a doctor.

"Well you know," said Doris, "I read somewhere that we don't choose our own crosses. God just lays crosses upon us in the midst of our attempts to serve. Through our struggles God is often at work molding us into the kind of person God wants us to be."

The Joy Of God

Dr. Yoshiro Ishida is an international church leader in the Lutheran Church. As his name may suggest Dr. Ishida is from Japan. He began his service to the church as a pastor in his church in Japan. He was spotted as a very promising young man and the church arranged for him to attend graduate school in the United States. He returned to Japan as a professor in the theological seminary.

After these years of service in Japan, Dr. Ishida was called to serve at the headquarters of the Lutheran World Federation in Geneva, Switzerland. He gave dedicated service to the global church in Geneva in a variety of positions. He was next called to head up a new "Institute of Global Mission" in Chicago, Illinois. Dr. Ishida and his American-born wife, therefore, moved to Chicago. Just a year ago he was called again, now almost at retirement age, to come back to Japan and help start a new four-year women's college.

Dr. Ishida's service to the global Christian community is a wonderful testimony to his dedication. But where did he get that faith? Dr. Ishida was born into a Buddhist family. He was raised in a land that is only about one percent Christian. How did the Christian message find him and bring him to faith?

A couple of years ago Dr. Ishida answered this question as he addressed a mission gathering here in the United States. Dr. Ishida told the group that he was a teenager during the Second World War. He came from a Buddhist family and he was quite devout. He spent much time at the Buddhist Temple in his city. The temple was a quiet place for meditation and devotion. It was a safe place. He liked being around the temple, he said. There was a security there for him as he gave expression for his need to be right with God.

Then one day at the temple, just by chance, he got his hands on a copy of the Christian Bible. There were many Bibles available in Japan even if there were very few Christians. So young Mr. Ishida began to read the Bible. It was a whole new world for him. At first he couldn't understand much of it at all. It didn't make that much sense. He couldn't figure out the point.

One day that all changed. The "scales fell from his eyes" we might say as he was reading Luke 15. It was the joy of God that really spoke to him. "My heart was caught with the fact that the parables portrayed the joy of God," he said to the hushed assembly. He recited a portion of the parables: "Just so, I tell you, there will be more joy in heaven over one sinner who repents than over 99 righteous persons who need no repentance. Just so, I tell you, there is joy in the presence of the angels of God over one sinner who repents." "Note this joy of God," he continued. "I couldn't believe it. I always thought *we need to get right* with God. That's what I was trying to do at the Buddhist Temple. But the Bible talked about a *God who needs to save us*. And when God saves us, when God finds us, God is filled with joy!"

" 'What a strange God this is!' I thought to myself. God is overjoyed with finding just one person. I found this new. I had never heard of such a thing. It meant that God was concerned with me. With me! Just one person! And God is filled with joy at finding me. To this very day, that is to me what the gospel of Jesus Christ is all about."

Final Payment

The story of Mary Gordon's book, *Final Payments* begins with a funeral. Isabel Moore's father was being laid to rest. Isabel had been the person solely responsible for taking care of her father since she was 19 years old. She was now 31. She had single-mindedly devoted her life to her father. People around Isabel Moore thought she was a saint because of her affection for her father.

But what do you do with your life when, at age 31, you are deprived of your sole reason for living? Isabel Moore had to invent a life for herself. Everything was new to her. Buying clothes, looking for a job, dealing with the house her father left her — all new! But Isabel Moore did get on with her life. She even fell in love with a veterinarian, Hugh Slade. Isabel found herself irresistibly drawn to this married man.

Hugh Slade's wife Cynthia, called an end to this affair. She confronted Isabel at a party. "You are a good person," Cynthia told Isabel. "Everyone says you are." She then proceeded to scold Isabel for her every action.

"Yes, I had been a good person," Isabel Moore thought to herself. It was as if Cynthia Slade's words had shocked her back into reality. She decided then and there that her affair with Hugh must end. "We are both good people," she told him. "We must not hurt anyone. We must not be selfish." Strangely enough, this woman who had devoted almost all her adult life to her father's care, found selfishness to be her greatest sin.

Isabel Moore next decided that she must atone for her selfishness and sin. She would be a good person again. She would be sacrificial again. She would give her life to the most undeserving person she knew. She would devote her life to Margaret Casey. Margaret Casey had been the housekeeper for Isabel and her father after Isabel's mother had died. Isabel was only two years old at the time. She grew up, therefore, under the watchful eye of Margaret Casey, a woman she despised. In fact, Isabel hated Margaret so much that when she was 13 years old she almost single-handedly dismissed her from her job as caretaker for her father.

In her attempt to be a good person again, however, Isabel saw Margaret as an unfinished debt she had to repay. "I would absorb myself in the suffering of someone I found unattractive," Isabel thought to herself. "It would be a pure act, like the choice of a martyr's death which, we had been told in school, is the only inviolable guarantee of salvation."

And Isabel did it. She cared for Margaret who paid her back only in spite. Margaret criticized Isabel's every move. Finally, Isabel could take no more. She sold her one possession, her house, and gave the money to Margaret. "I left on the table in front of Margaret a check for $20,000. It was all the money I had in the world. But I was free of Margaret now. I felt weightless . . . ."

It is from this action that the novel gets its title. This was Isabel Moore's *final payment*. She felt bound in guilt over the way she had treated Margaret. She had a ransom to be paid in order to buy her own peace of mind. Isabel's act is a universally human act! Because of the selfishness of our deeds we all feel a need to make a final payment, to pay a ransom that will purchase our peace with God.

Proper 21
Luke 16:19-31

Hear No Evil . . .

Narrative Analogy: *Luke 1:46-55 (53); 4:18-16; 19:1ff; 16:14-15 et al*

Remains Of The Day is a powerful movie starring Anthony Hopkins and Emma Thompson. Hopkins plays the role of the chief butler at a large estate in England. Emma Thompson plays his chief assistant. The movie is set in the years immediately preceding and succeeding World War II.

The butler is the central figure in the film. He has come by his trade naturally. His father was a butler before him. The estate, therefore, is the only home he has ever known. He knows no other life. In this world he is a man of absolute dependability. He runs the large estate staff like clockwork. He is a model of efficiency. He is also a man who seems to have no emotions whatsoever. One evening, for example, while the staff is busily serving a marvelous banquet the butler is called aside. His father, who also works and lives at the estate, has taken ill. The butler goes quietly to his father's room. He finds his father is dying. He takes care of matters quite efficiently and goes back to the demands of the banquet. Not a tear is shed.

The head of the estate in these pre-war years in England is a man who has great sympathy for the German cause. Many meetings are held at his estate as he seeks to enlighten others in the cause of his sympathy. Much pro-Nazi discussion takes place around the ornately crafted tables of the estate. The butler is right there in the midst of all this. He hears the discussions but it seems to make no impression upon him whatsoever.

After the war the butler receives a warm letter from the woman who had in years past been his chief assistant at the estate. This was a woman who was greatly attracted to the butler. The butler either did not notice her attraction to him or he did not know how to comport himself in the presence of this beautiful woman. No one had ever taught him about love. At any rate, in response to her letter the butler gets the use of one of the cars of the estate to go and visit her with an eye to hiring her back to her old position. Watching the movie one hopes that, at long last, love will come to full bloom between these kindly souls. The entire movie works to build our suspense about this matter. She sends out all the clues in the world to him that she is interested more in him than in a position at the estate. But the butler cannot hear. The butler cannot see.

On his way to speak with his former assistant his car breaks down. He finds himself waiting for help at a local pub. The patrons of the pub ask where he is from. He mentions the estate. At first they mistakenly assume that he might own the estate. They ask him many questions. He can answer none of them. Two distinguished looking gentlemen get into the discussion with the butler. They have sized him up as a common man. They ask him his impressions of the former head of his estate. "Do you agree with the positions of your master?" they inquire. "What do you think of the war?"

The questions totally confuse the butler. "No, I don't have an opinion on that. No, I don't understand that." Those who have put the questions to him laugh at this common man who understands nothing. Just as they thought! The audience is left puzzled. The butler has heard many discussions at his master's estate concerning the war. He has been there. He has heard. He has seen. But he has heard and seen nothing. The butler cannot hear. The butler cannot see.

Gospel Grandmothers

United Church has a tradition. They were known for supporting their pastors very well. Any pastor who has ever served at United will verify the truth of this tradition. Pastors, for example, consider it a privilege to serve in this congregation deep in the heart of Texas. Pastor Mike Snyder surely did. Pastor Mike, as everyone called him, had had a kind of love affair with this congregation throughout his nine years of service at United. The feeling was mutual. The people of United felt uniquely blessed by him as well.

It was not much of a surprise, therefore, when the church board at United decided to hold a special evening meeting to honor and celebrate the ministry of Pastor Mike Snyder. Someone on the board had found out that this year was the 25th anniversary of Pastor Snyder's ordination. Everyone agreed immediately that there should be a party, a Texas-style party to honor their pastor's 25 years of ordained ministry. And so it was.

The party for Pastor Snyder's anniversary was held on a hot Texas summer night. Just about the whole congregation turned out for it. Choirs sang their favorite numbers. The younger children recited verses of Bible stories they had learned. One of the members of the high school youth group spoke on their behalf. Many adults spoke as well. There was a representative of the women's organization, the men's club, the church board and just about every other group at United.

In their speeches people took care not to paint Pastor Snyder as some kind of perfect saint. It wasn't that Pastor Snyder's ministry with them was without fault. In fact, they knew his faults pretty well. There were some well-timed jokes concerning the fact that Pastor Snyder often neglected his own family in order to get all the ministry done at United. "You have to find more time for your own family," said the woman from the women's organization. Other jokes teased Pastor Snyder about the short fuse on his temper. They reminded him gently to put a lid on it!

And so the party went on. Words of thanksgiving and praise were spoken. So were words of caution and concern. And now it was time for Pastor Snyder's response. Jimmie Jones, chair of the church board, invited the pastor to the podium. "One of the things you've done best among us," said Jimmie, "is to help bring faith to life. We'd like to know who helped you. Who helped you to faith, Pastor Mike?"

"My grandmother," said Pastor Snyder without hesitation. "I believe that my grandmother had a tremendous shaping power over my life of faith even though I never knew her. She died eight years before I was born. But I heard the stories. I heard stories of how she headed up the Sunday school until she died. I heard stories of how she was the pioneer in seeing to it that the English language was introduced into her congregation of immigrants. I heard many stories of her faith."

"I can't explain it but I have always felt that my call to the ministry was a call to fulfill my grandmother's legacy. In some mysterious way I feel that her vision of Christian service has been passed along to me. She is, in a very special way, my 'gospel grandmother.' I'll bet many people here tonight can name a 'gospel grandmother' who has helped to lead you to faith. I thank God, we should all thank God, for our grandmothers in the faith!"

Proper 23
2 Timothy 2:8-15

God Is Faithful To Godself

His hands were surely trembling as he lifted his hammer to nail his theses to the door of the Castle Church in Wittenberg, Germany. The year was 1517. The man was Martin Luther. Luther had lived through many a crisis in his personal relationship to God. Out of his struggles he came to believe that much of what his church had taught him was simply wrong. It was wrong teaching that had caused his faith crisis.

Luther decided to go on the offensive. The topic for his offensive was the matter of "indulgences." The Christian church at the time of Luther believed that sins committed after one was baptized that were not specifically forgiven would have to be paid off in purgatory. Purgatory was understood to be the place where souls lived after their death and before their resurrection. An indulgence from the church freed one from punishment in purgatory for a prescribed number of sins. Luther accepted some of this belief but he was enraged when he discovered that the church was actually selling "full indulgences" to people while asking nothing from them in terms of repentance and new life. This Luther protested. He nailed his *95 Theses* for debate on the matter to the Castle Church door.

Think about this! One man. One man stands up to challenge a fundamental teaching of his church. Who did he think he was anyway? What gave him the courage to carry out his convictions in this way?

Thanks to the new media of print, Luther's *95 Theses* were spread all over Europe. The church was not pleased. They tried to curb Luther in a variety of ways. They even declared him to be excommunicated from the church. The matter came to a head several years later in a meeting held in the city of Worms, Germany. The meeting was called a "Diet." It was a meeting of none other than the Holy Roman Empire which governed most of Europe in those days. It was presided over by the Emperor, Charles V, himself. Before this incredible display of political and churchly power Luther was asked two questions. All of his writings were placed on a table in the center of the room. "Did you write these books?" he was asked. And a second question: "Would he recant any of what he had written?"

Luther was forced into a corner. The answer he gave is perhaps the best known words he ever spoke. He would not recant. "Here I stand," he said finally. "I can do no other. God help me! Amen."

And again we ask: how could one man have the courage of convictions so that he might stand against the Holy Catholic Church and the Holy Roman Empire? Luther, himself, gives us an answer to our question. A year later he preached a series of sermons in his home church in Wittenberg. To the question, "How did you do this?" Luther replies, "I did nothing." Here are his words: "I simply taught, preached, and wrote God's Word; otherwise I did nothing. And while I slept, or drank Wittenberg beer with my friends Philip and Amsdorf, the Word so greatly weakened the papacy that no prince or emperor ever inflicted such losses upon it. I did nothing; the Word did everything!"

What gave Luther his courage? His confidence was in the Word and promises of God. He simply believed that God is always faithful to God's promises. God cannot deny Godself. Even though we be faithless, God will be faithful. That's where Luther stood!

Proper 24
Jeremiah 31:27-34

A New Heart

Narrative Analogy: *Jeremiah 11:1-17; 32:26-44*

It was the religious program she had heard on the radio a few weeks back that sent Shawn Rose on a mission to her pastor. Shawn had been a solid church-going member all of her life. She took her faith seriously. She had taken it seriously already in her Sunday school years. In high school, too, she really tried to live out the truth of her religious belief in the midst of incredible peer pressure to do otherwise.

Shawn's growing up years tested her faith conviction a lot but nothing prepared her for the difficulty of living out her faith as an adult. Shawn wanted desperately to be obedient to her Lord's demands upon her life. Deep inside herself, however, she knew that she was not living up to the letter of the law. In personal relationships, in business relationships and in just plain living she found that she just did not measure up to God's standards. Something was horribly wrong, she thought.

And then she heard this religious radio program sponsored by her denomination that had simply pushed her over the edge. It was a sermon centered on the words God spoke to Jesus when Jesus was baptized by John the Baptist. God said to Jesus: "You are my Son, the Beloved, with you I am well pleased" (Luke 3:22). The content of the sermon was basically that God was pleased with Jesus because Jesus truly did God's will. "If we do God's will," the pastor had said, "then God will speak words of favor to us as well."

"I didn't like that sermon at all," Shawn told Pastor Chung.

"Well it sounds all right to me," Pastor Chung responds. "What is it that you don't like?"

115

"I don't know," Shawn replied. "Something is just not right here. Look, I've been trying all my life to do God's will and please God. I think when I was younger I actually believed I could do it. God's will, I mean. I would just put my mind to it and be obedient. I'm not so sure about that any more. Maybe I'm the only one in your congregation who has this problem but, quite frankly, there are just too many times when I don't do God's will as I understand it. Is there something wrong with me?"

"I suppose what's wrong with you is that you are a sinner," Pastor Chung offered softly.

"Yeah," said Shawn, "that's what I've heard here all of my life. Yet, in spite of all the sermons that I've heard, all the teaching and all the Bible that I've read, nothing in me changes very much. What I've heard doesn't seem to have taken very deep root. I hear, but I do not do."

"I'm sure you can do better, Shawn," Pastor Chung said assuredly.

"Well I'm not so sure I can do better," Shawn Rose shot back almost in anger. "Do better, do better, do better! It seems that's all I've heard my whole life. And I've tried. God knows I've tried. But I don't get any better. In fact, I think I'm getting worse."

"You really have to dig deep inside yourself to get this right," declared her pastor.

"But that's where the problem lies," Ms. Rose protested. "How can my inner self be the solution when that's where the problem is? You know what? I need a new answer to my question. Something new has got to happen to me. I think what I really need is a new heart."

Proper 25
Luke 18:9-14

Ready For Worship

Narrative Analogy: *Luke 10:29-37; 16:14-15*

Ernie, Madge and Todd Applegate always took their place in a front pew just as the bell was ringing. The Applegates were regular and faithful members of the First Church of Christ. They knew what to do once they got into their pew. Each head bowed as the Applegates silently prepared themselves for worship.

Ernie Applegate thought long and hard that morning about a matter that haunted him a bit. He and his boyhood friend Phil Crane had both been candidates for a new position at the telephone company where they had worked together since high school days. Both men really wanted this new position. In his interview with the company, Ernie had said some things about Phil that he had never told anyone before. Ernie hated to do it and his conscience bothered him a bit, but this new position meant everything to him and his family.

The way Ernie had it figured, he certainly needed the position worse than Phil did. Phil's wife, after all, had a full-time job. The Cranes had two incomes. Madge only had a part-time job at a dress shop. That was simply not enough extra dollars to support their daughter in her first year of college. That reality had put a real crunch on their budget. It's true. He probably shouldn't have said what he said about his good friend. On the other hand, he had plenty of *justification* for it. Ernie's meditation ended there. He was ready for worship to begin.

While Ernie was meditating on his life in preparation for worship, his wife did likewise. Something haunted her, too. Madge had been working part-time at a new dress shop in town for about eight months now. The shop was owned and operated by Susan Glenn. Actually, Madge Applegate had never really trusted Susan Glenn all that much but the job was posted; she needed work; she took the job. It didn't take many days in the shop for Madge to be reminded why she didn't trust Ms. Glenn. Her boss marked up almost every item in the dress shop a full 20 percent over the suggested retail price. That bothered Madge. She felt guilty charging folks, many of whom were her friends, an outlandish price for their purchases.

Then one day a good friend of Madge came into the store to look at dresses. She found just the dress she wanted but the price was just too high. Right then and there Madge Applegate instituted a new policy unbeknownst to her boss. She cut the price by 20 percent. Her friend was so happy that she gave Madge a tip for her kindness. Now this caused a whole new scheme to develop at Susan Glenn's dress shop. Many women in town soon realized that for a small tip, Madge Applegate would cut 20 percent off the price of almost everything in the shop.

As Madge prepared for worship this Sunday morning she thought about the plan she had devised. On the one hand, she knew she shouldn't be doing it. But, on the other hand, her boss was not being fair to the customers in her pricing policies. As for the tips Madge received, she judged that to be all right in light of the extra business it produced. Madge's meditation for this Sunday was now over. She concluded, as she usually did, that she was *justified* in her deeds. Madge, too, was ready for worship to begin.

"Who Can Be Saved?"

Narrative Analogy: *Luke 1:46-55 (52-53); 6:20-26; 12:13-31;
16:1-15, 19-31*

"Zacchaeus was a wee little man, a wee little man was he
....'' Many people have learned that song in Sunday school.
We might be tempted to think, therefore, that this is a story
"for children only." Nothing could be further from the truth.
The story of Zacchaeus is one of the most important stories
for children and adults in the entire Gospel of Luke. It's important because it tells us how Christians can live with wealth.
It's important because the story of Zacchaeus tells how it is
that we can be saved.

Zacchaeus was a man who gouged his riches out of his people in the form of additional taxes. He was a man hated by
the people of Jericho. Zacchaeus was a sinner. He had broken
most of the laws of his people. Zacchaeus stands quite in con-
trast to a rich young ruler whose story Luke has just told (Luke
18:18-30). The rich young ruler is a righteous man. He has
kept most of the laws of his people. He is beloved by the people of his town.

And so, one day, Jesus came to the town of the rich young
ruler. The ruler had a question for Jesus. "... what must I
do to inherit eternal life?" the ruler said to Jesus (Luke 18:18).

Jesus answered the rich ruler. "You know the commandments," Jesus said. "You shall not murder; You shall not steal;
You shall not bear false witness; Honor your father and
mother" (Luke 18:20).

If you had been there just then you would have seen a
big smile break out all over the rich ruler's face. He was
tickled to death. He'd done all this! He had kept all the

commandments! "I have kept all these since my youth," he said to Jesus through his broad smile (Luke 18:21). This was a man who had just found out that he would be saved. His deeds made it so.

But Jesus wasn't finished with the rich young man. "Not so fast," Jesus seems to say. "There is still one thing lacking. Sell all that you own and distribute the money to the poor, and you will have treasure in heaven; then come, follow me" (Luke 18:22).

The smile immediately left the young man's face. He was very rich. There was just no way that he was going to give up all his wealth. Not even for his salvation. Jesus reflected upon his departure: "How hard it is for those who have wealth to enter the kingdom of God!" (Luke 18:24).

Now there was a crowd observing all this. They were scandalized by Jesus' words and the ruler's departure. They knew this young man. They knew him to be an upright and honest man. They knew him to be a benefactor of the town. "If this man can't be saved," they said to Jesus, "then who can be saved?"

Jesus replied: "What is impossible for mortals is possible for God" (Luke 18:27). This is a wonderful, high-sounding answer to the question of the crowd. But what does it mean? What does it mean for you and for me? If a wonderfully righteous person like the young ruler can be turned away from salvation, what hope is there for us? None of us lives up to the standards of the rich young ruler. None of us has kept all the commandments. Is salvation a possibility for us at all?

"Who then can be saved?" Luke's answer: Zacchaeus can be saved! Sinners can be saved! "What is impossible for mortals *is* possible for God." "For the Son of Man came to seek out and save the lost" (Luke 19:10).

"You Are God"

Out On A Limb, Shirley MacLaine's spiritual odyssey, was first published in 1983. She calls this book her unfinished spiritual diary. In her book Ms. MacLaine joins forces with the Sadducees of old and with many, many people in our land today, who do not believe in the resurrection of the dead. MacLaine's replacement for a belief in the resurrection is a belief in *reincarnation*. Reincarnation asserts quite simply that we don't need to be raised from the dead because we never die. Only our body dies. Our true inner self continues to live forever inhabiting many bodies along the way.

In her book MacLaine tells of an evening she spent with a man by the name of Kevin Ryerson. Kevin Ryerson was a *channel* so that people who did not occupy a body could speak to the living. Through Kevin Ryerson, as MacLaine tells it, a person named John spoke to her. MacLaine actually claims to have taped their conversation. One of the first things John told her was that, "... to understand the soul within yourself today, you must also understand something of previous civilizations you have known ... you were incarnate several times during the 500,000-year period of the most highly evolved civilization ever known to man" (p. 197-198).

John preceded to tell Ms. MacLaine that she lived twice before as a male and once as a female. He told her that Gerry, a politician from England with whom she had an instant affinity and an affair, was her soul mate. "Soul mates," John said, "were actually created for one another at the beginning of time ..." (p. 200).

John also instructed Ms. MacLaine in the reality of extraterrestrials who can teach us true knowledge. "The only important knowledge," John went on to tell her, "is the spiritual knowledge of God within every man. Every other knowledge flows from that" (p. 200). It wasn't difficult for MacLaine to figure out that if we are really God then, of course, we can never die. God doesn't die. I am God. I don't die. We don't need a resurrection! This she learned from John.

John even talked to Shirley about the truth of the Bible. He warned her though that the Bible had been badly misinterpreted through the years. "Reinterpreted by whom?" MacLaine asked. "Ultimately by the church," John reported. "It is to the advantage of the church to 'protect' people from the real truth ... (which is) the process of each soul's progression through the ages. The real truth being each soul's responsibility for its own divinity."

"You mean reincarnation," MacLaine interjected.

"That is correct," John affirmed. "The church wishes to deny you this truth, '... because such a truth would make the power and the authority of the church unnecessary. Each person, that is, each entity, becomes responsible to its self for its conduct' " (p. 204-5).

John then reaffirmed his basic teaching, "the big truth." "*You* are God," he told MacLaine. "*You* know you are Divine. But you must continually remember your Divinity and, most important, *act* accordingly" (p. 209).

Shirley MacLaine, and many like her in our world today, do not believe in the promise of resurrection given by Jesus. Self-proclaimed gods, after all, live forever. They don't need any help with matters of life and death.

122

A Vision For The Future

More than the past

A few years back a west coast bishop returned home from a meeting of his denomination's bishops in Kansas City. He reported on the meeting to his staff. He worked up the most energy in talking about the three major speakers. "One of the speakers," he told his staff, "teaches Bible at one of our seminaries. She did an excellent job of tracing all the currents of biblical research that have brought us to the present. She gave an excellent review of the recent and not so recent past in biblical studies."

"A second speaker," the bishop continued, "was a theologian. He did much the same thing as the biblical teacher. He reminded us of our heritage. He talked about the giants of theology in the early 20th century. He outlined the major streams of theology that have brought us to our present state."

The bishop started warming to his subject now. "The third speaker," he reported with a gleam in his eye, "was an incredibly gifted lay woman who works in the field of applied science. She is a member of our denomination and a product of one of our church colleges. The things she told us about the nature of science today were mindboggling. It's a field that is changing with incredible speed. The average length of time of a job in her field is three years. The average length of time of a company in the field is seven years. On the one hand, she said, that is scary. On the other hand, however, this is probably the most exciting time to be alive that humankind has ever known. Things are changing. There are grand new opportunities. We can change our future!"

After he had finished reviewing the speakers the bishop grew more serious. "I found it interesting," he went on, "that our church's teachers talked to us mostly about the past while she talked to us mostly of the future. And that's not all. She not only talked about the future but she made it clear that science has moved far beyond the point of thinking that God is to be factored out of any intelligent equation. As we move to a new future, she said that the spiritual issues were of absolutely vital concern. And you have the answers here, she said to us. We look to you. We need you. Help us provide the spiritual sustenance the world needs as we move toward a new tomorrow."

The bishop was clearly fond of this woman scientist. He had a chance to visit with her at the end of the five days they were together. He reported to his staff on that conversation as well. "She told me," the bishop began, "that she had been very carefully observing our group over our five days together. And she was impressed. 'These are wonderful leaders,' she told me. 'As a group you are incredibly bright and talented. I've never heard any group that is so knowledgeable of the kind of issues you discuss with each other. I've been listening in on your conversations and I am thankful that my church has such dedicated leaders. But,' she said, 'everything you talk about is in the past. It's the past that you are so expert in discussing. It's the church's past that you are so knowledgeable of. But I don't think I've heard anyone discuss the future. Where is your church going in this exciting time? What kind of new future are you going to create? Surely in the church you have language to talk about the future. Surely you have language in the Bible which can hold out a vision of hope for a new world.' "

Christ The King
Luke 23:33-43

"Jesus, Remember Me"

Narrative Analogy: *Luke 3:21-22; 9:18-22, 28-36*

Sheila Stone had had the respect of everyone in her community. She was one of the pillars of her congregation. She had served on the city council longer than anyone in the history of her small town. She was a caring, decent person. Everyone knew that. What everyone didn't know was that her personal life was a different story. Sheila's husband was the main culprit here. He was a businessman who just wasn't very good at business. People in town knew that he went from one business to another. That was obvious. What was not so obvious was that his businesses were financial disasters. Ed and Sheila Stone were in debt up to their eyeballs. And it wasn't just Ed's debts that had them buried in bills. Both of their girls had attended expensive private church colleges. Sheila thought her daughters just must get this kind of education in order to have a shot at a good future.

But how to pay the bills? Sheila Stone found a way. She had worked at Citizen's National Bank for years. She had been the chief financial officer of the bank for the past ten. And Sheila did the unthinkable. She was sure she could doctor the books of the bank in such a way that her embezzling enterprise would never be discovered. She was wrong. It was discovered. Sheila Stone went to prison for ten years for her crime.

Sheila wept when she talked to her friends after the trial. "What have I done?" she cried out to them. "How could I have ever thought that I could get away with this? I knew it was wrong. I've disgraced myself, my friends, my church and my God. Whatever will become of me?"

Buck Schwartz was Mr. Athletics in his home town of Maplewood. He had been a great athlete in high school in many sports. He went to college not so far away from home and his hometown folks followed his career there with interest and pride. The hometown boy had, indeed, made good. After Buck's graduation from college no one was surprised when it was announced that he would come back home as a coach.

Buck started his coaching career as the assistant football coach and the head track coach. Football was what Buck was primarily known for and it wasn't many years before he became head coach in that sport. He coached his teams to title after title. Everyone loved Buck Schwartz. He was an institution in his own hometown.

And then the accusations started to fly. One woman claimed that she was pregnant with his child. Another claimed the same thing had happened to her years before though she never made the news public. The people of Maplewood were shocked. They couldn't believe their ears. No one had any idea that "Coach Buck" was that kind of man. He did seem to be happily married, after all. He was active in his church. How could this be? "Coach Buck" asked the same question. He didn't understand himself. "How can this be?" he confided to his pastor. "What's wrong with me? Where will I end up anyway?"

"Whatever will become of me?" said Sheila Stone. "Where will I end up anyway?" said Buck Schwartz. Here are two people who had lost their way in life. Two people who had forgotten who they were. Two people who had forgotten their Lord. Would the Lord also forget them? Or, would the Lord remember?